PENGUIN CLASSICS

THE SOCIAL CONTRACT

JEAN-JACQUES ROUSSEAU was born in Geneva in 1712. Orphaned at the age of ten he tried his hand as an engraver's apprentice before he left the city in 1728. From now on he was to wander Europe seeking an elusive happiness. At Turin he became a Catholic convert; and as a footman, seminarist, music teacher or tutor visited many parts of Switzerland and France. In 1732 he settled for eight years at Chambéry or at Les Charmettes, the country house of Madame de Warens, remembered by Rousseau as an idyllic place in the *Confessions*. In 1741 he set out for Paris where he met Diderot who commissioned him to write the musical articles for the *Encyclopédie*. In the meantime he sired five children by Thérèse Levasseur, a servant girl, and abandoned them to a foundling home. The 1750s saw mounting quarrels with Voltaire and Diderot, and his writing struck a new note of defiant independence. In his *Discours sur les sciences et les arts* and the *Discours sur l'origine de l'inégalité* he showed how the growth of civilization corrupted natural goodness and increased inequality between men. In 1758 he attacked his former friends, the Encyclopedists, in the *Lettre à d'Alembert sur les spectacles* which pilloried cultured society. In 1757 he moved to Montmorency and these five years were the most fruitful of his life. His remarkable novel, *La nouvelle Héloïse* (1761), met with immediate and enormous success. In this and in *Émile*, which followed a year later, Rousseau invoked the inviolability of personal ideals against the powers of the state and the pressures of society. The crowning achievement of his political philosophy was *The Social Contract*, published in 1762. That same year he wrote an attack on revealed religion, the *Profession de foi du vicaire savoyard*. He was arrested but fled to England where he only succeeded in making an enemy of Hume and returned to his continental peregrinations. In 1770 Rousseau completed his *Confessions*. His last years were spent largely in Paris and he died in 1778.

•

MAURICE CRANSTON was born in 1920 and educated at London University and Saint Catherine's, Oxford. He was a part-time lecturer at London University from 1959 to 1969 and since 1969 has been Professor of Political Science at the London School of Economics. In 1978 he was seconded as Professor of Political Science to the European University Institute. His many publications include *Human Rights Today* (1954), *A Glossary of Political Terms* (1966), and *The Mask of Politics* (1973). His biography of John Locke won the 1957 James Tait Black Memorial Prize. Professor Cranston is married and has two sons.

Jean-Jacques Rousseau

THE SOCIAL CONTRACT

TRANSLATED
AND INTRODUCED BY
MAURICE CRANSTON

PENGUIN BOOKS

Penguin Books Ltd, Harmondsworth, Middlesex, England
Viking Penguin Inc., 40 West 23rd Street, New York, New York 10010, U.S.A.
Penguin Books Australia Ltd, Ringwood, Victoria, Australia
Penguin Books Canada Limited, 2801 John Street, Markham, Ontario, Canada L3R 1B4
Penguin Books (N.Z.) Ltd, 182–190 Wairau Road, Auckland 10, New Zealand

—

This translation first published 1968
Reprinted 1969, 1970, 1971, 1972, 1974, 1975, 1976, 1977, 1978,
1979, 1980, 1981, 1982, 1983 (twice), 1984, 1985, 1986 (twice), 1987

—

—

Made and printed in Great Britain by
Hazell Watson & Viney Limited,
Member of the BPCC Group,
Aylesbury, Bucks
Set in Monotype Bembo

CONTENTS

TRANSLATOR'S ACKNOWLEDGEMENTS

The translator wishes to acknowledge the debt he owes to various friends and Rousseau specialists who have helped him to deal with the problems he has met in attempting to put this text into intelligible English. He is especially grateful to Professor James Burns, Baron Bertrand de Jouvenel, Professor Robert Derathé, Mr R. A. Leigh, Mr John Charvet, Professor John Weightman and Mr William Pickles.

INTRODUCTION

THE *Social Contract* is, as Rousseau explains in his preface, a fragment of something much more ambitious – a comprehensive work on *Institutions politiques* which he began to write in 1743 but never finished. In 1743 Rousseau was thirty-one years old, and working as private secretary to the Comte de Montaigu, French Ambassador to the Venetian Republic. This place gave Rousseau his first intimate acquaintance with politics and government. The Ambassador was a retired general with no qualifications or aptitude for diplomacy. Rousseau, who was quick and capable, and could speak Italian, performed the duties of Embassy Secretary. Unfortunately, he had no official status; he was not a diplomatist; he was the Ambassador's personal employee; he was, as the Ambassador tactlessly reminded him from time to time, a domestic servant. Rousseau felt cheated and humiliated. To do the work of a diplomatist and be treated like a lackey was unbearable.* Within a year, he was gone, dismissed, and not even given his promised wages.

What made the Comte de Montaigu's attitude the more unbearable to Rousseau was not only the injustice, but also the underlying reality: Jean-Jacques *was* a servant, and he had never been anything much better. He had the soul and the mind, as the whole world was soon to recognize, of an exceptional and superior being, but his rank and condition were humble. He had been born in Geneva on 28 June 1712, the second son of Isaac Rousseau, a spirited and irresponsible watchmaker of that city. His mother died a few days after

* Indeed Voltaire put about the false story that Rousseau had been the Ambassador's valet, not his secretary. For evidence of Rousseau's duties at the Embassy see R. A. Leigh, ed., *Correspondance complète de Jean-Jacques Rousseau*, Geneva, 1965 (hereinafter abridged as *Corr. complète*), vols. 1 and 2.

giving him birth. He was brought up, together with his elder brother, by an aunt and a nurse maid. Isaac Rousseau, who had a passion for books, entertained his sons by reading them novels, histories and the heroic biographies of Plutarch, so that Rousseau could afterwards boast, 'I was a Roman before I was twelve.' In fact, by the time he was ten, the readings from Plutarch had come to an end; his father had fought a duel which obliged him to quit Geneva, and the sons were boarded out with a Calvinist pastor and his sister. At the age of thirteen Rousseau was apprenticed to an engraver, at whose house he lived.

'My trade,' he recalled many years later, 'did not displease me in itself. ... I should perhaps have succeeded if the brutality of my master and excessive constraint had not disgusted me with the work.'*

Rousseau's very first taste of employment was thus to him an experience of bondage. He had grown up in greater freedom than most children. He had been petted, even spoiled by his father and by the several women who did their best to make up to him for the loss of his mother. Besides, as one of his biographers has noted, Rousseau belonged to a family which had come down in the world, and in his early years 'he suffered from a kind of social down-grading which he was to spend his whole life trying to rectify'.† His father had failed as a watchmaker partly because he was too cultured a man for an artisan's trade and partly because he had not enough strength of character to make the best of his situation. Isaac Rousseau lived in a world of fantasy, he wasted the legacy his wife had left him, and he was finally forced into exile because he insisted on settling a dispute by a 'gentleman's' appeal to the sword. In some ways, perhaps, he was like his son.

* Quoted by Jean Guéhenno in *Jean-Jacques Rousseau*, trans. J. and D. Weightman, London, 1966, vol. I, p. 15.
† op. cit., p. 14.

One Sunday evening in March 1728, when he was not yet sixteen, Rousseau found himself shut out of Geneva after a walk in the country; he had forgotten the time, and the city gates were closed when he reached them. This had happened to him twice before, and his master had beaten him for staying out all night. This time he decided he would not go back at all.* So his life of wandering began.

In the Catholic principality of Savoy, surrounding the city of Geneva, priests were on the look-out for converts among the young people who came from that Calvinist republic. Not only priests; there were proselytizers also among the laity, including a remarkable woman of thirty, the Baroness de Warens, who lived, separated from her husband, at Annecy and specialized in helping young men. It was to Madame de Warens that Rousseau was sent by the first Catholic friend he made in Savoy. To his surprise, she was agreeably unlike the usual charitable lady of the parish. 'What I saw was a face that was charm itself; beautiful, blue eyes, full of sweetness; a ravishing complexion; the curve of an enchanting bosom.'† Madame de Warens was a romantic as well as a pious woman. Her religious sentiments were never perhaps wholly distinct from erotic feelings; one form of ecstasy merged easily into another; but if her converts and her protégés were sometimes also her lovers, her connexion with the priests protected her from scandal. She even received from the King of Sardinia a pension in recognition of her work for the salvation of young Protestant souls.

Madame de Warens did not immediately detain Rousseau at Annecy. She urged him on to Turin, where he was to renounce his Protestant faith and lodge in a Catholic hospice.

* Less perhaps because he feared a beating than because he yearned for adventure. See Georges May, *Rousseau par lui-même*, Paris, 1963, p. 8.

† *Confessions*. See *Œuvres complètes*, Bibliothèque de la Pléiade, Paris, 1959–65 (hereinafter abridged as 'Pléiade'), vol. I, p. 49.

Then to earn his keep he was obliged to become a footman. He disliked the experience and, remembering Madame de Warens, went back to Annecy the following summer to seek her patronage. This time she took him into her household and mothered him; he called her *maman* and she called him *petit*. She also arranged for him to have music lessons, and so provided the training for what was sometimes to prove his chief means of earning a living, a bearable alternative to domestic service: work as a music copyist and music teacher.

Madame de Warens also gave Rousseau access to a substantial library, and thus enabled him to educate himself from books. From time to time, Rousseau wandered away from Madame de Warens' house, working for other employers, travelling in search of adventures, seeking his identity,* but he always returned to what was the only home he had. When he was twenty, Madame de Warens decided, as Rousseau puts it, 'to treat me as a man'. The affair lasted for six years; then Rousseau discovered that Madame de Warens had taken another lover, one Winzenried. Gradually, Rousseau's life ceased to centre on her house in the Savoy. While working as a tutor in the family of Monsieur de Mably, brother of the socialist theorist, the Abbé de Mably, Rousseau conceived the idea of becoming a writer, and this ambition prompted him to seek his fortune in Paris.

Rousseau's first problem as a budding writer was to discover the medium in which to express what he had to say. He had never any doubt that a writer's mission was to give verbal expression to the truth; at the same time he felt that the truth was melancholy and disturbing. He had also the familiar problem of a livelihood. When music copying and music lessons did not bring in enough, he became private secretary to another benefactress, Madame Dupin, wife of a rich tax-

* This last was perhaps a life-long quest. See R. Grimsley, *Jean-Jacques Rousseau, A Study in Self-awareness*, University of Wales Press, 1961.

farmer. It was through this connexion that Rousseau gained the opportunity to enter what he visualized as the more distinguished world of diplomacy as secretary to the French Ambassador in Venice.

The year in Venice was miserable. The Comte de Montaigu and his secretary got on one another's nerves. Rousseau became increasingly bitter as he felt more exploited, deceived and abused. The Ambassador found Rousseau impudent, churlish and hysterical. They parted, each thinking the other mad and each accusing the other of robbing him. Besides, Rousseau did not much care for Venice or the Venetians. Architecture did not appeal to him, and Venice lacked nature. Its famous courtesans did not provide the kind of love he wanted; one of them advised him to give up women and study mathematics. His chief consolation was the Italian opera, which he adored. As a republican city-state he considered Venice much inferior, politically, to his native Geneva, but at least the comparison prompted him to start writing what he himself regarded as his most important book:

Of the different works that I had on the stocks [he wrote long afterwards in his *Confessions*] the one ... at which I worked with the greatest liking, to which I wished to dedicate myself all my life, and which, in my belief, was to set the seal upon my reputation, was my *Institutions politiques*.... I had come to see that everything was radically connected with politics, and that whatever was done about it, no nation would be other than what the nature of its government made it....*

After the interlude in Venice, Rousseau made his way back to Paris. He was still angry and indignant about the way he had been treated, but once in Paris his fortunes began to change. He had already made friends with an enterprising contemporary, another young man who had come up from

* Pléiade, vol. 1, p. 404.

the provinces, Denis Diderot, and the two of them talked of taking the literary world of France by storm. Their dreams were extravagant, but in the event their success was far greater than anything they contemplated. Rousseau first made his mark as a musician. He invented a new system of musical notation. It was not accepted by the Academy, but it gained him an award. His *Dissertation sur la musique moderne* was published, and attracted notice. He also composed operas and ballets in the Italian style. His ballet *Les Muses galantes* was performed in Paris in the autumn of 1745, and enjoyed some success in spite of the open scorn of Rameau, the leading French composer of the time. Rousseau's opera *Le Devin du village* was played at Fontainebleau in 1752 before a delighted audience which included the King. Rousseau might then have had a Royal pension, but, torn by conflicting emotions, longing for the money but proud and contemptuous of kings, he let slip the opportunity.

Diderot in the meantime was making his name as the editor of what was to prove the most significant literary enterprise of eighteenth-century France, the great *Encyclopédie*. All the leading French intellectuals or *philosophes* contributed to Diderot's pages. Rousseau, too, was a contributor, writing at first on musical and afterwards on other subjects. He found the work difficult. 'I am worn out,' he wrote to Madame de Warens, 'but I have given my promise and one must keep one's word. Besides, I want to get at the throats of people who have treated me badly, and bile gives me strength, even intelligence and knowledge.'*

The *Encyclopédie* got Diderot into trouble. He was more of an atheist than Voltaire; he had been trained for the priesthood as a young man, and his anti-clerical materialism had the

---

* Rousseau to Madame de Warens, 27 January 1749, *Corr. complète*, vol. 2, p. 113. Among the throats Rousseau aimed at was that of the composer Rameau.

sharp edge of apostasy. Under pressure from the religious authorities, Diderot was imprisoned in July 1749 at Vincennes. One memorable afternoon, Rousseau went to visit him there. According to the story Rousseau tells in his *Confessions*, he had a singular experience on the journey. He opened a copy of the *Mercure de France* and read the announcement of a prize essay competition on the question 'Has the revival of the arts and sciences done more to corrupt or purify morals?' Rousseau tells us that it came to him as a sudden revelation what the answer was. Hardly able to breathe, let alone walk, he sat under a tree and wept. When he reached Vincennes, he told Diderot what had happened. His friend encouraged him to enter for the essay competition, and uphold the opinion that the revival of the arts and sciences had only corrupted morals. Diderot did not agree with this at all, but he was a born journalist, and he suggested that such an unfashionable belief would distinguish Rousseau from the other competitors and capture the prize. Diderot was right. Rousseau submitted his essay and won; henceforth, whether he liked it or not, he was a famous man.

The subject of the Dijon essay was nicely designed to make Rousseau realize how different from other men's his opinions were, different not only from those of the majority, but from those of Diderot and the other *philosophes* of the Enlightenment. Whether it all came to him suddenly on the road to Vincennes or whether the thoughts had been slowly maturing in his head for years, Rousseau had now worked out a *Weltanschauung* which was distinctively his own, and which put him at odds with all the prevailing streams of eighteenth-century opinion, both religious and materialistic.

Diderot and the other *philosophes* were all disciples of the English philosopher Francis Bacon. They believed in progress: more precisely they believed that the development and organization of empirical knowledge could immeasurably improve the life of man on earth. Science would save us. Two steps were needed to realize this project. First, superstition must be banished; traditional philosophy, that unscientific amalgam of Christianity and Aristotle, must be swept away to clear the path to real knowledge. Secondly, the pursuit of such real or empirical knowledge had to be planned, for the conquest of nature was not something that one individual philosopher could accomplish alone in his study; it could only be done by research undertaken by scholars in cooperation. The *Encyclopédie* itself was an example of such collaboration, with experts in different fields each helping to provide a synopsis of all available knowledge. The object was not merely an academic one; as Diderot wrote in the preface to the first volume: 'Our aim is to gather all knowledge together, so that our descendants, being better instructed, may become at the same time happier and more virtuous.'*

Rousseau, in his first prize essay, attacked all these Baconian notions. Science was not saving us; it was bringing moral ruin on us. Progress was an illusion. What appeared to be advancement was in reality retrogression. The development of modern civilization had not made men either happier or more virtuous. Happiness belonged to man's life in a state of nature. Virtue was possible in a simple society, where men lived austere and frugal lives. In modern sophisticated society man was corrupted, and the greater the sophistication the greater the corruption.

The arts of civilized societies served only to 'cast garlands of flowers over the chains men bore'. The sciences were the fruit of their vices. Arithmetic, for example, sprang from avarice; physics from idle curiosity; mechanics from ambition. And this evil in the origin of the sciences appeared again in their purposes. If men were not unjust, they would have no use for jurisprudence; if there were no wars or conspiracies or tyran-

* *Encyclopédie*, vol. 1, Préface.

nies, there would be no history. Error was unfortunate, but ignorance did no harm. As for the grand Baconian hope of creating abundance on earth, Rousseau saw more evil than good in it. Abundance to him spelt luxury, and luxury was notoriously a breeder of corruption. Frugality, he argued, was equally necessary for a good and upright life in an individual and for a strong and healthy state. Luxury undermined nations as it undermined men.

As an example of a frugal nation Rousseau mentioned Sparta. Throughout his life he continued to regard Sparta as an ideal model of the city-state. Athens he admired less. For Athens had an advanced and sophisticated culture; it made itself a seat of politeness and taste, a city of poets and orators, its buildings as elaborate as its literature. All these Athenian arts and sciences, Rousseau argued, went with moral decay, and he quoted the authority of the Athenian Plato to support him: for had not Plato said that so-called scientific knowledge was not knowledge at all and proposed that poets and artists should be banished from an ideal republic?

To Diderot, a cheerful and tolerant man, these arguments of Rousseau were so many entertaining paradoxes, not to be taken too much to heart. He was inclined to regard them as the product of Rousseau's Swiss origins. Rousseau's love of Sparta and dislike of Athens he saw as an expression of his attachment to Swiss rusticity and estrangement from French civility. And indeed Rousseau's 'rusticity' grew more pronounced when, as a result of winning the Dijon prize, he became a celebrity, and the fashionable hostesses of Paris began to vie with one another for the honour of entertaining him in their *salons*. Diderot, like the other *philosophes*, relished such social success. Rousseau did not. He could get on well with titled ladies on a basis of intimate friendship; Madame de Warens was only the first of a succession of noblewomen who responded to Rousseau's charms and put themselves out to befriend him. But he was painfully ill at ease in the *salons*, in social gatherings that were governed by intricate rules of behaviour. Lacking the appropriate upbringing, Rousseau was paralysed by what he afterwards called a 'false shame'. Refusing to play the part of a literary celebrity in Paris, he began to live what he spoke of as 'a life of solitude'.

He did not, however, live entirely alone. Soon after he returned from Venice to Paris he formed a union with an unusually ignorant laundry-maid named Thérèse le Vasseur, and thereafter she and her mother were part of his permanent household. Thérèse bore him five children, who were all dispatched to an orphanage as soon as they were born. Late in life Rousseau married her. Possibly it was another sign of what Diderot called his 'Swiss rusticity' that the same Rousseau who fled from the *salons* could feel at home in a kitchen with a girl who was backward and stupid and plain.

Switzerland had undoubtedly affected his thinking. In one of his polemical writings* Rousseau recalled how, as a youth, he had been impressed by a village that stretched up a mountainside near lake Neuchâtel. There, he said, was a community of little wooden houses, each standing in the centre of the piece of land on which the family depended. Each was about the same size. It was a community of equals. The inhabitants were happy peasants, unburdened by taxes and tithes, who supported themselves by their own work. They were all skilled in a great variety of trades; there was no cabinet-maker, locksmith, glazier or carpenter among them, because every man did such work for himself. They built and maintained their own houses. They also provided their own amusements; they could all dance, sing, and play the flute. Moreover,

---

* *J.-J. Rousseau, Citoyen de Genève, à M. D'Alembert . . . sur le Projet d'établir un théâtre de Comédie en cette Ville* in *Collection complète des Œuvres de J.-J. Rousseau*, Geneva, 1782, vol. II.

Rousseau added, their taste – unlike that of modern townsfolk – was good.

Rousseau recalled this mountain community in the course of a controversy with D'Alembert, co-editor with Diderot of the *Encyclopédie*, when D'Alembert had proposed that Geneva should improve its amenities by building a theatre. Rousseau replied protesting, first, that dramatic performances were morally harmful, and secondly, that a healthy culture had no need of theatres. The example he gave of such a sound culture was, significantly, not Geneva itself, but this rural Swiss community which had kept its simplicity, and still lived much as it had lived for hundreds of years; it had been spared the corrupting influence of 'progress'.

Neuchâtel was politically a protectorate of the Prussian crown; in other Swiss cantons the rustic culture went together with a form of primitive democracy which held for Rousseau a peculiar interest. These cantons were sovereign political societies united in a loose confederation with their neighbours. They were small enough to have the whole adult male population meet at intervals to legislate. This was democracy somewhat on the lines of that of the ancient Greek city-states, and it was something which survived in Europe only in Switzerland. Allemanic democracy was at least as old as Tacitus, who considered it a typically tribal and barbaric institution. It was a form of government which could only go together with a simple form of culture, a small state, a face-to-face society where everyone knew his neighbours, and where all men were more or less equal.

In other parts of the western world, democracy came to be seen as a progressive, liberal idea; the champions of democracy in America, France and elsewhere were men who wanted to democratize parliamentary or representative government by introducing universal suffrage. The democrats of rural Switzerland had no need to be reformers. They had democracy already, and their only problem was to keep it. The notion of 'representation' was alien to their direct democracy where *every* citizen was a legislator. Indeed, progressive, liberal ideas were seen as a threat to Swiss democracy, for they went together with the movement to centralize Switzerland, to set up a national parliament, and merge the independence of the cantons in a large modern state. Democracy in rural Switzerland went logically together with a conservative, even a reactionary disposition; and it should not astonish us to find in Rousseau a similar belief in legislation by the citizens *en masse* coupled with hostility to progressive and liberal opinions.*

In 1754, when he was forty-two, Rousseau wrote a second essay for the Academy of Dijon. This one, which failed to win the prize, was on the question: 'What is the origin of inequality among men, and is it authorized by natural law?' What he wrote had more bearing on the first part of the question than it had on the second. His *Discours sur l'origine de l'inégalité parmi les hommes* is largely historical; the question of right and law he reserved for the *Social Contract*, and by the time he came to write the later work his views had to some extent changed.

In the *Discours sur l'inégalité* Rousseau depicts the state of nature as one of innocence. What distinguishes men from beasts is first their faculty of self-improvement and secondly man's only natural moral quality, which is compassion or sympathy. In the state of nature, man lives alone. It is when he becomes sociable that he becomes wicked. In the early stages, when each begins working together with other men in

---

* 'When we see among the happiest people in the world bands of peasants regulating the affairs of state under an oak tree, and always acting wisely, can we help feeling a certain contempt for the refinements of other nations, which employ so much skill and mystery to make themselves at once illustrious and wretched?' (*The Social Contract*, Book IV, Chapter 1.) The Swiss cantons are not named, but the reference is obviously to them.

hunting or in joint defence against natural disasters, association sharpens man's feelings of sympathy, and so breeds
notions of consideration and obligation. But other things also
happen. The cultivation of the earth leads to the enclosure of
land, and this necessarily gives rise to the idea of property. As
Rousseau puts it in a famous sentence: 'The first man who,
after fencing off a piece of land, took it upon himself to say
"This belongs to me" and found people simple-minded
enough to believe him, was the true founder of civil society.'*

Rousseau explains what he means in this way: once men
begin to claim possessions, the inequality of men's talents and
skills leads to an inequality of fortunes. Wealth enables some
men to enslave others; the very idea of possession excites
men's passions, and provokes conflict. Society breeds war.
This leads in turn to a demand for a system of law to impose
order and tranquillity. The rich especially voice this demand,
for while the state of violence threatens everyone's life, it is
worse for the rich because it threatens their possessions also.
Hence the agreement between men to live under a political
system.

Such was, or may have been, the origin of civil society and laws,
which gave new fetters to the poor, and new powers to the rich;
which destroyed natural liberty for ever, fixed for all time the law of
property and inequality, transformed shrewd usurpation into settled
right, and to benefit a few ambitious persons, subj~cted the whole of
the human race thenceforth to labour, servitude and wretchedness.†

The effect of the establishment of political societies is both
to institutionalize and increase inequalities. The establishment
of such things as property rights and titles of nobility sets the
seal of law on inequality. But 'even without the intervention
of government, inequality of credit and authority became

* Pléiade, vol. 3, p. 164.
† ibid., p. 178.

unavoidable among private persons as soon as their union in the same society led them to compare themselves one to another'.* In the end society reaches a point where men come to be satisfied with themselves rather on the testimony of other people than on their own. Where the savage 'lives within himself', the social man 'lives constantly outside himself, and only knows how to live in the opinion of others; he acquires, so to speak, the consciousness of his own existence only from the judgement of others'. †Rousseau suggests, however, that things need not have turned out as badly as they have. If, with the establishment of government, men 'ran headlong into chains', that was because men had the sense to see the advantages of political institutions, but not the experience to foresee the dangers. To this theme Rousseau was to return some years later in the *Social Contract*.

When the *Discours sur l'inégalité* was published in September 1755 it carried a dedicatory epistle to the Republic of Geneva, a fulsome tribute to the author's native city:

Having had the happiness to be born among you, how could I meditate on the equality which nature has set between men and the inequality which they themselves have instituted, without reflecting on the profound wisdom by which equality and inequality, happily combined in that Republic, are balanced in the manner that is most in conformity with natural law, and most favourable to society, to the maintenance of government and to the happiness of individuals.‡

This gesture was one of Rousseau's manoeuvres to recover his rights as a citizen of Geneva. Already at the age of fifteen he had proudly scribbled his name on a country gate: '*Jean-Jacques Rousseau, citoyen de Genève, 1727.*' As the son of a citizen he would normally have been entitled to become one also, but when he adopted the Catholic faith in Savoy, he forfeited the right, and it was only when he formally returned

* Pléiade, vol. 3, pp. 188–9.   † ibid., p. 193.   ‡ ibid., p. III.

to the Calvinist fold that he was able to regain it. His association with Thérèse made the Protestant pastor hesitate to administer Holy Communion, but Rousseau protested that Thérèse was only his servant, and in his dedicatory epistle to the Republic of Geneva he went out of his way to proclaim his belief in chastity: 'Lovable and virtuous daughters of the city, it will always be the destiny of your sex to govern ours. Happy we are, so long as your chaste power, exercised solely within the marriage tie, is exercised only for the glory of the state and the happiness of the people.'* Rousseau had not yet put his own union with Thérèse 'within the marriage tie'; but he could plausibly argue that the disease by which he was increasingly afflicted – a constriction of the bladder which forced him to wear a catheter – disabled him from fornication.

Rousseau's stay in Geneva was brief, and any illusions he may have had of finding a congenial form of government in that city were soon removed. Seven years later, when his *Social Contract* and *Émile* were published, both books were burned by the government of Geneva and a warrant issued for the arrest of the author, notwithstanding the fact that the *Social Contract* contained several flattering references to Geneva, notably in the preface to Book I where Rousseau writes: 'Whenever I reflect on governments, I am happy to find that my studies always give me fresh reasons for loving that of my own country.'

It is not difficult to imagine why the *Social Contract* offended the authorities of Geneva. In theory the city was a republic, and the *Social Contract* is an intensely republican book. But in practice Geneva was a patrician gerontocracy, dominated by a few families. It was an example of what is castigated by Rousseau as the worst form of constitution, that is one in which the sovereignty has passed from the people into the hands of an hereditary aristocracy.

* ibid., p. 119.

The twelve years between the winning of the Dijon prize for his *Discours sur les sciences et les arts* when he was thirty-eight and the publication of the *Social Contract* when he was fifty formed the most creative period of Rousseau's life, in spite of the fact that he suffered during this same period from almost constant pain because of the urinary disease. He worked on *Émile* and his novel, *La Nouvelle Héloïse*, at the same time as he was working on the *Social Contract*. In the same twelve years he wrote, besides his *Discours sur l'inégalité* his *Lettre à D'Alembert sur les spectacles*, his attack on the stage, his *Lettre à Voltaire sur la providence*, a defence of religious faith as a rejoinder to Voltaire's *Poème sur le désastre de Lisbonne*; he wrote his *Lettre sur la musique française* to promote the natural melodic style of Italian music against the intellectual, artificial French style (and particularly against the music of Rameau); and he wrote his *Essai sur l'origine des langues*, applying to the theory of communication ideas which he had elsewhere applied to the theory of art.

During these productive years, Rousseau had lived in the country some little distance from Paris, first at L'Hermitage, a cottage in the park of Madame d'Épinay, and afterwards at Montmorency, on the estate of another patron, the Maréchal de Luxembourg. He was deeply wounded when Diderot, as he imagined, mocked him for leading this secluded way of life: 'Only the bad man lives alone,' says a character in Diderot's play, *Le Fils naturel*.* In any case, Rousseau's rural peace came to an end in 1762, when *Émile* was condemned by the *parlement* of Paris, and the author had to flee from France to avoid arrest. He went to Bernese territory in Switzerland, where he learned that he was a wanted man in Geneva as well as in France. Then he was expelled from the canton of Berne. He had offended almost everyone: Catholics, Protestants,

---

* For Diderot's version of the story see A. M. Wilson, *Diderot*, O.U.P. 1957, pp. 254ff. The incident led to a final rift between the two writers.

materialists. And so, the last unhappy phase of his life began, when, as the victim of political and religious intolerance, he was harried from place to place in search of refuge.

*

The political views of the *philosophes* were as distasteful to Rousseau as were most of their opinions. Like their master, Francis Bacon, they believed in strong government; the doctrine of planning called for a ruler with enough power to put plans into effect; and just as Bacon himself once dreamed of converting James I to his way of thinking and then using magnified royal prerogative to enact his proposals, so the *philosophes* of the eighteenth century based their hopes for success on influencing powerful monarchs to do what they suggested. The current name for this was *le despotisme éclairé*; to Rousseau, the champion of freedom, any kind of despotism was anathema, and the so-called enlightened sort seemed rather worse than others.

In 1755 Rousseau addressed a letter to a pastor in Geneva who had conceived the idea of launching a literary periodical: 'Believe me, Sir, this is not the sort of work for you,' he wrote. 'Serious and profound writings may do us credit, but the glitter of that trivial philosophy which is fashionable today is wholly unbecoming to us. Great themes such as virtue and liberty enlarge and fortify the mind; little things, like poetry and the fine arts, give it more delicacy than subtlety.'*

The great themes of liberty and virtue were the themes of the *Social Contract*. This is why Rousseau attached so much importance to the book; and also, perhaps, why it got him into trouble. It might seem to the reader that Rousseau started to write the *Social Contract* as a book about liberty and ended up with a book about virtue; in truth it is the argument of the

* Rousseau to Jacob Vernes, 2 April 1755. Quoted in Georges May, op. cit., p. 26.

whole book that once men have entered into society, freedom comes to be inseparable from virtue.

Some time between the writing of the *Discours sur l'inégalité* and the writing of the *Social Contract*, Rousseau read the works of Thomas Hobbes. His only reference in the *Social Contract* to Hobbes are fleeting and hostile ones, but Professor Robert Derathé* has shown that Rousseau was not in the habit of acknowledging his intellectual debts, and that his debts were particularly great both to the legal theorists, or jurisconsults, of earlier generations, to Grotius,† Pufendorf,‡ Barbeyrac,§ and Burlamaqui,‖ and also to the political philosophers, especially Hobbes and Locke. The second title of Rousseau's *Social Contract* is the same as the main title of one of Burlamaqui's books: *Principes du droit politique*. This *droit politique*, which I have been obliged for lack of a better alternative (there is no English equivalent of *le droit*) to translate as 'political right', Burlamaqui employed as a semi-technical expression to designate the general abstract study of law and government, and Rousseau uses the word in the same sense.

The main title of Rousseau's *Social Contract* refers to a concept which all these jurisconsults and political philosophers invoked. They all believed that the state was the outcome of a covenant or agreement among men. The purpose of the state was the protection of those people to which it owed its being, and the same theorists also agreed that the sovereign must have enough power to provide such protection. Most of

* *Jean-Jacques Rousseau et la science politique de son temps*, Paris, 1950.

† Hugo Grotius (1583–1645), Dutch jurist; author of *De jure belli et pacis* (1625).

‡ Samuel Pufendorf (1632–94), German jurist; author of *Elementa jurisprudentiae universalis* (1660), *De jure naturae et gentium* (1672), *De officio hominis et civis* (1673).

§ Jean Barbeyrac (1674–1744), French jurist, translator and commentator on the works of Grotius and Pufendorf.

‖ Jean-Jacques Burlamaqui (1694–1748), Genevan jurist; author of *Principes du droit naturel* (1747), *Principes du droit politique* (1754).

the theorists sought at the same time to limit this power of sovereigns under one principle or another, and even to divide sovereignty between several elements. Hobbes stood apart from the others in insisting that sovereignty must be unified and absolute. Hobbes said that men must choose: either they were ruled or they were free; they could not be both; liberty went with anarchy and security with civil obedience.

Rousseau accepted Hobbes's argument on one point; he agreed that sovereignty must be absolute or nothing, but he could not bring himself to accept Hobbes's notion that men must choose between being governed and being free. Rousseau, who loved liberty so much, believed he could show that it was possible for men to be at once free and members of a political society. Indeed the *Social Contract* may be read as an answer to Hobbes by an author whose mind was stimulated by the brilliance of Hobbes's reasoning, but who could not stomach Hobbes's conclusion.

It is important to note what Rousseau is doing in the *Social Contract*. He explains it clearly at the beginning: 'My purpose is to consider *if*, in political society, there can be any legitimate and sure principle of government, taking men as they are, and laws as they might be.' The *if* is crucial. Rousseau is not offering a plan for reform,* nor is he writing the kind of history and sociology he provides in his *Discours sur l'inégalité*. He is dealing with *right* rather than with *fact*, though fact comes into it, because he undertakes to deal with men 'as they are'. In the *Social Contract* Rousseau is dealing, in the hypothetical mood, with abstract problems which seem to him to emerge from philosophical reflection on the actual nature of man and the possible order of laws and government. The social contract discussed in the *Social Contract* is not the actual

---

* Rousseau deals with practical politics in his *Projet de Constitution pour la Corse* (written 1764–5) and his *Considérations sur le gouvernement de Pologne* (written June 1771).

historical contract described in the *Discours sur l'inégalité*, that *imposture** made to consolidate the advantages of the rich. It is a genuine and legitimate contract, which is to the benefit of everyone, since it unites liberty with law and utility with right.

Now Rousseau not only rejects Hobbes's claim that men must choose between being free and being ruled, he positively asserts that it is only through living in civil society that men can experience their fullest freedom. This is the connexion between freedom and virtue. Here we may detect a modification of the argument of the *Discours sur l'inégalité*. In the earlier work Rousseau stresses both the freedom and the innocence of man in the state of nature. In the *Social Contract* he still says that men have freedom in the state of nature, but he treats it as freedom of a crude and lesser kind. Such freedom is no more than independence. And while he does not accept Hobbes's picture of man in the state of nature as an aggressive and rapacious being, Rousseau (having read Hobbes) speaks less of the innocence and more of the brutishness of man in a state of nature. Man in the state of nature, as he is depicted in the *Social Contract*, is a 'stupid and unimaginative animal'; it is only by coming into a political society that he becomes 'an intelligent being and a man'. Assuredly, as a result of the growth of passions and sophistry which society breeds, men have generally grown worse with the passage of time; but that is because society, instead of improving men, has corrupted them. Society is bound to change men, and if it does not do what it is meant to do, and improve them, it will worsen them. Nevertheless, according to Rousseau, it is only by leaving the state of nature and becoming a social being in the fullest sense, that is to say, in becoming a citizen, that man can realize his own nature as man.

* For a discussion of this see J. Starobinski, 'Du Discours de l'inégalité au Contrat social' in *Journées d'Étude sur le Contrat Social*, Paris, 1964.

Rousseau never abandons the belief, put forward in his *Discours sur l'inégalité*, that men are happy in the state of nature. He continues to think it possible for them to be good. Men cannot, however, be virtuous in the state of nature, virtue being a characteristic of men who are conscious of morality. Unlike Hobbes, Rousseau does not suggest that it is fear which drives men to quit the state of nature; but he does say that it is man's weakness which makes him social.* Rousseau also suggests both that Providence has to intervene by creating natural disasters and shortages to force men to cooperate and also that there is a certain natural pressure within men to actualize those social and moral qualities which are mere potentialities in a state of nature.

Here one might suspect a certain equivocation in Rousseau's use of the word 'nature'. But what he is saying is that the state of nature is man's *original* state, not his natural state; for man can only realize his full nature as a man by making the social compact and living under law. Rousseau's ambiguity reflects a common ambiguity in the word 'nature', which is sometimes used to refer to what is, and sometimes to refer to what should be. Rousseau uses the word 'nature' at different times in either of these two senses.

In a way, Rousseau's solution to the problem posed by Hobbes is wonderfully simple. Men can be both ruled and free if they rule themselves. For what is a free man but a man who rules himself? A people can be free if it retains sovereignty over itself, if it enacts the rules or laws which it is obliged to obey. Obligation in such circumstances is wholly distinct from bondage; it is a moral duty which draws its compulsion from the moral will within each man. In this argument, we can detect a striking departure from the 'social contract'

---

* 'It is the weakness of man which renders him social: it is our common, miseries which carry our hearts towards humanity.' *Émile*, Book IV, p. 249 Paris, 1524.

theorists who preceded Rousseau. The jurisconsults and Hobbes and Locke all rejected the well-established theories that sovereignty was based on nature or on divine right, and they all argued in one way or another, that sovereignty derived its authority from the assent of the people. But these earlier theorists also held that sovereignty was transferred from the people to the ruler as a result of the social contract. Rousseau is original in holding that no such transfer of sovereignty need or should take place: sovereignty not only originates in the people; it ought to stay there.*

Rousseau's solution to the problem of how to be at the same time ruled and free might plausibly be expressed as democracy. I have already spoken of the importance to him of what is commonly named 'democracy' in Switzerland. But Rousseau himself used the word 'democracy' in a rather distinctive fashion,† because of the emphasis he puts on the difference between the two departments, as he sees them, of government. Ruling, in the strict sense of making rules or laws, is the function which he says that the people must retain; for thus, and only thus, does sovereignty express itself. Every act of the sovereign is a law, and anything which is not a law is not an act of sovereignty. From this function of law-making, Rousseau distinguishes the administration, or executive management, of government. And he does *not* demand, as a prerequisite of liberty and legitimacy, that this administration shall be conducted by the whole body of citizens. On the contrary, he thinks it might be best done by a limited number. The conduct of administration by the whole body of the citizens he seems to consider too utopian an arrange-

* See Derathé, op. cit., p. 47.

† In a letter to Madame d'Épinay, dated March 1756, Rousseau wrote: 'Learn my dictionary, my good friend, if you want to have us understand each other. Believe me, my terms rarely have the ordinary sense.' Quoted in C. W. Hendel, *Citizen of Geneva: Selected Letters of Jean-Jacques Rousseau*, New York, 1937, p. 140.

ment. And this is the arrangement which in the *Social Contract* he calls 'democracy', and of which he is thinking when he says that democracy is for gods, not men.*

Rousseau is undoubtedly a democrat in the sense that 'democracy' means legislative rule by the whole body of the citizens; but as he himself used the word in another sense, it might be less confusing to speak of him as a 'republican' or champion of 'popular sovereignty'. One of the reasons why he distinguishes so carefully between the legislative sovereign body and the executive or administrative body is his consciousness of the abiding danger to the legislative which the administrative body constitutes. For while it is convenient that the business of government should be entrusted to a council of magistrates or commissioners, those magistrates will naturally tend, with the passage of time, to encroach on the sacred territory of legislation, and thus to invade the sovereignty and destroy the republican nature of the state. As a matter of empirical fact, Rousseau even suggests that this is bound to happen.†

Nowhere in the *Social Contract* does Rousseau offer any

---

* See Book III, Chapter 4.

† Bertrand de Jouvenel has drawn attention to a contradiction here between Rousseau as a philosopher and Rousseau as a political scientist. Rousseau the political philosopher argues that legitimate government is possible only if sovereignty remains in the hands of the citizens. Rousseau the political scientist puts forward as an empirical law of development that the executive or administrative body must in the long run invade the legislative body and capture the sovereignty. Jouvenel cites a passage from Rousseau's *Lettres écrites de la montagne* (Part 1, Letter 6): '... since sovereignty tends always to slacken, the government tends always to increase its power. Thus the executive body must always in the long run prevail over the legislative body; and when the law is finally subordinate to men, there remains nothing but slaves and masters, and the republic is destroyed.' Jouvenel stresses that the 'must' in this paragraph is a scientific must; so that Rousseau the political scientist is denying the possibility of the continued existence in the real world of the one form of political association which unites liberty with government. See B. de Jouvenel on 'Rousseau' in *Western Political Philosophers*, ed. M. Cranston, London, 1964, and Jouvenel's introduction to his edition of *Du Contrat social*, Geneva, 1947.

short definition of liberty, although there are several often-quoted epigrams about it. In his *Lettres écrites de la montagne* (published two years after the *Social Contract*) he provides the most succinct account of what he means by this key word:

Liberty consists less in doing one's own will than in not being subject to that of another; it consists further in not subjecting the will of others to our own. . . . In the common liberty no one has a right to do what the liberty of any other forbids him to do; and true liberty is never destructive of itself. Thus liberty without justice is a veritable contradiction. . . . There is no liberty, then, without laws, or where any man is above the laws. . . . A free people obeys, but it does not serve; it has magistrates, but not masters; it obeys nothing but the laws, and thanks to the force of the laws, it does not obey men.*

It is partly because of this intimate connexion between liberty and law that the freedom of man in a state of nature is so inferior. The freedom of the savage is no more than independence; although Rousseau speaks of the savage being subject to natural law, he also suggests that the savage has no consciousness of natural law; thus Rousseau can speak of a man being 'transformed', as a result of his entry into civil society, from a brutish into a human, moral being. A moral being is, or can be, free in another sense than the political; if, instead of being a slave of his passions, he lives according to conscience, lives according to rules he imposes on himself, then he has a liberty which only a moral being can enjoy. The savage has no sense of this; for one thing, the passions only begin to develop with society, which explains why society can mark the beginning of a change for the worse as well as the beginning of a change for the better. One of the new passions which emerges with society is pride or *amour-propre*, which Rousseau sees as an evil mutation of the perfectly innocent sentiment of self-love or *amour-de-soi*. It is a

* *Lettres écrites de la montagne*, Letter 8, Pléiade, vol. 3, pp. 841-2.

characteristic of modern sophisticated culture to be dominated by pride. The emphasis on 'going back to nature' in Rousseau's treatise on education, *Émile*, is the result of his belief that cultural environment, not natural inclination, breeds such harmful passions. Here we may notice a contrast between Rousseau's views and Hobbes's. Whereas Hobbes holds that pride is natural to man, Rousseau holds that it is artificial; whereas Hobbes says that war prevails among men in the state of nature because of men's pride, Rousseau says that war is a product of conflicts about property, and therefore cannot exist in the state of nature, where there is no property.

On the other hand, Rousseau seems to be entirely at one with Hobbes when he says that under the pact by which men enter into civil society everyone makes a total alienation of all his rights. However, it must be remembered that Rousseau regarded this alienation as a form of exchange, and an advantageous one; men give up their natural rights in exchange for civil rights; the total alienation is followed by a total restitution; and the bargain is a good one because what men surrender are rights of dubious value, unlimited by anything but an individual's own powers, rights which are precarious and without a moral basis; in return men acquire rights that are limited but legitimate and invincible. The rights they alienate are rights based on might; the rights they acquire are rights based on law.

It might be supposed that Rousseau is contradicting Locke when he says that men alienate all their rights when they make the social contract, Locke having said that men make the social contract only to preserve their rights. But Rousseau is really thinking in different terms from Locke. Rousseau does not think that men have in the state of nature the kind of natural rights which Locke supposes – the right, for example, to property. For Rousseau there is only *possession* in the state of nature; property (by definition, rightful possession) comes into being only when law comes into being. Nor does Rousseau think, like Locke, of liberty as one of men's rights. Indeed he says, quite as emphatically as Locke, that men *cannot* alienate their liberty. If Locke and Rousseau were thinking in the same terms, it would be a contradiction for Rousseau to say, as he does, that the social contract entails the total alienation of rights, and that men cannot alienate their liberty. In truth, what Rousseau is saying is that instead of surrendering their liberty by the social contract, they *convert* their liberty from independence into political and moral freedom, and this is part of their transformation from creatures living brutishly according to impulse into men living humanly according to reason and conscience.

There is no more haunting paragraph in the whole of the *Social Contract* than that in which Rousseau speaks of forcing a man to be free.* But it would be wrong to put too much weight on these words, in the manner of those who consider Rousseau, whether early-fascist or early-communist, at all events a totalitarian.† Rousseau is nothing so simple. He is authoritarian, but the authority he favours is explicitly distinguished from mere power; it is based on conscious and vocal assent, and is offered as something wholly consistent with liberty. There is no necessary antithesis, as some writers assume, between liberty and authority as such; for authority is a form of potency which rests on the credence and acceptance of those who respect it, and Rousseau insists that if authority is to be legitimate the credence and acceptance must be both universal and unconstrained. There is no resemblance between Rousseau's republic and the actual systems of twentieth-century totalitarian states, where the various devices of party rule,

* Book I, Chapter 7.
† See, for example, J. L. Talmon, *The Origins of Totalitarian Democracy*, London, 1952. For a rejoinder to Talmon see R. A. Leigh, 'Liberté et autorité dans le Contrat social' in *Jean-Jacques Rousseau et son œuvre*, Paris, 1963.

government by edict, brain-washing and secret police are manifestations of what Rousseau regarded as despotism and vigorously condemned. Indeed for those who seek the theoretical ancestry of present-day totalitarian ideology, the optimistic *despotisme éclairé* of the *philosophes* may well be worth as much attention as the pessimistic republicanism of Rousseau.

Rousseau does not say that *men* can be forced to be free in the sense that a whole community may be forced to be free; he says that *a* man may be forced to be free, and he is thinking here of the occasional individual who, as a result of being enslaved by his passions, disobeys the voice of the law, or of the general will, within him. The general will is something inside each man as well as in society as a whole, so that the man who is coerced by the community for a breach of the law, is, in Rousseau's view of things, being brought back to an awareness of his own true will. Thus in penalizing a law-breaker, society is literally correcting him, 'teaching him a lesson' for which, when he comes to his senses, the offender should be grateful. Legal penalties are a device for helping the individual in his own struggle against his own passions, as well as a device for protecting society against the anti-social depredations of law-breakers. This explains the footnote to Chapter 2 of Book IV of the *Social Contract*, where Rousseau writes: 'In Genoa the word *Libertas* may be seen on the doors of all the prisons and on the fetters of the galleys. This use of the motto is excellent and just.'

In arguing thus, Rousseau may be seen as adopting and elaborating an argument used by Locke against Hobbes. Hobbes in his plain, robust way, says that to be free is to be unopposed and unconstrained in doing what one wants to do; the law is a form of constraint, so that the less the law forbids, the more free a man is: 'The liberty of the subject is the silence of the laws.' Locke rejects this; he holds that the law does not diminish men's freedom, but effectively enlarges

35

it, both by protecting a man from anarchic invasions of his liberty and by preventing collisions between one man's use of his liberty and another's. Locke even accepts the notion, though he never uses the words, of forcing a man to be free, because he mentions the case of a man who is prevented by *force majeure* from crossing a bridge which is dangerous and which he does not know to be dangerous; as soon as the man learns the true situation, he is grateful to those who have taken hold of him, and no longer feels that his freedom has been invaded. This is the kind of situation that Rousseau has in mind – albeit on a much larger scale – when he speaks of forcing a man to be free. The recalcitrant, to Rousseau, is someone who is out of joint with himself and with society, and thus to use physical restraint on him is not to harm, or injure, him, but, on the contrary, to help or heal, to recover him for reason, and therefore, at the same time, for freedom. It is difficult, assuredly, to reconcile this way of thinking with Rousseau's partiality for the death penalty.

In the discussion of liberty, Rousseau's whole emphasis is different from Locke's. Locke is not worried, as Rousseau is, by corruption; and he does not hanker after virtue. Locke thinks that a system of positive law set up by a constitutional state can enlarge men's liberty, but he also thinks that many systems of positive law do diminish men's liberty. For Locke there are good laws and bad laws. Good laws are the ones that recognize and defend men's natural rights, bad laws are the ones that neglect or abuse those rights. And therefore for Locke the problem is to have positive laws that secure men's rights and avoid laws that imperil men's liberty. But Rousseau has a different approach, or rather he has two distinctive approaches to law. When he is speaking of law as right, a law, for him, is by definition just; and even when he characterizes a law as an expression of the general will, it is still by definition just because the general will is by definition righteous. But, secondly, when Rousseau is thinking about the kinds of law he sees in the real world, when he is thinking, so to speak, as an empirical social scientist, he notes that all actual systems of law can be seen to be unjust. In a footnote to Book IV of *Émile* he writes: 'The universal spirit of laws in all countries is to favour the stronger against the weaker, and those who have against those who have nothing: this disadvantage is inevitable and without exception.'*

There is thus for Rousseau a radical dichotomy between true law and actual law, between law as it should be and law as it is seen in the existing world. And it should not be forgotten that the law he is writing about in the *Social Contract* is law in the true sense. Thus laws, as he explains them in these pages, are rules made by a people in its capacity of sovereign and obeyed by the same people in its capacity as subject. Rousseau thinks it axiomatic that such rules will never be oppressive for the simple reason that a people, being at the same time sovereign and subject, would never forge fetters for itself. The only thing he fears is that the people, being ignorant, might forge fetters unwittingly: hence the need for the lawgiver.

The distinction between true law and actual law corresponds to the distinction Rousseau draws between the general will and the will of all. The general will is a normative concept, its connexion with right is a matter of definition. The will of all is an empirical concept; the only test of the will of all is what, in fact, all will. Having been so severe on Grotius for failing to distinguish between fact and right, Rousseau is careful not to make the same mistake himself.

Why should I abide by the decision of the majority? Because by the deed of the social contract itself, to which *everyone* subscribes and pledges (there is no question of a majority here; you either subscribe or you are not in civil society

* *Émile*, Classiques Garnier, Paris, 1924, p. 270.

at all), everyone agrees to accept the decision of the majority in the formulation of the law. But it is also understood that the members of the majority whose decision is accepted do not ask themselves what do *I*, as an individual, demand, but what does the general will demand; thus it is the majority *interpretation* of the general will which is binding and not the majority will. This is how it can be morally obligatory for the minority to accept.

Rousseau borrows from Hobbes the argument that sovereignty is an absolute power; it cannot be divided and remain sovereign; and it cannot be subject to 'fundamental laws' and remain sovereign. At the same time Rousseau takes from Locke and the jurisconsults the notion that sovereignty is limited. Sovereignty is absolute, but not unlimited. The limits are those imposed by natural law and by the considerations of public good. 'Sovereignty does not pass the bounds of public advantage.' As an example of what Rousseau means by a natural law limitation, we may note his argument in the *Social Contract* that no agreement to enter into slavery could be a valid one because any agreement which is wholly to the advantage of one party and wholly to the disadvantage of the other is void in natural law.

Several commentators, including C. E. Vaughan,* say that Rousseau eliminates natural law, but Professor Derathé has drawn attention to certain passages from Rousseau's writings which illustrate the importance he attaches to natural law. Derathé quotes Rousseau's claim, in the course of his controversy with D'Alembert, that he recognizes three authorities higher than the sovereign authority of the state: 'that of God, that of the natural law which derives from the constitution of man, and that of honour'.† Again, in the *Lettres écrites de la*

---

* C. E. Vaughan, *The Political Writings of Jean-Jacques Rousseau*, Cambridge University Press, 2 volumes, 1915.

† Derathé, op. cit., p. 157.

montagne Rousseau writes: 'It is no more permissible to violate natural law by the social contract than it is permissible to violate positive law by private contracts.'* Thirdly, in his *Considérations sur le gouvernement de Pologne* (written in 1771), Rousseau speaks of '... Natural law, that holy imprescriptable law which speaks to the heart and reason of man. ...'†

Against all this, it must be noticed that Rousseau in the *Social Contract* offers no possibility of an appeal to natural law. It is all very well to say, as he does, that the sovereign must not violate natural law, but this raises the question of who is to be judge of any such violation. In several of his writings, Rousseau emphasizes the supremacy of the individual conscience; he even goes so far as to speak of conscience as infallible. 'Conscience never deceives us.'‡ This might lead one to expect that he would agree with those theorists who hold that the individual conscience must ultimately decide where to draw the line between justice and injustice. In fact, in the *Social Contract* Rousseau takes up the position of Hobbes, namely, that the citizen can have no other guide but the civil law and the public conscience. The general will is itself the arbiter of just and unjust. Here there seems to be a contradiction between the argument of the *Social Contract* and that of the *Profession de foi* and other writings. In the *Social Contract* the general will is the moral authority; elsewhere individual conscience is represented as the innate principle of justice.

This points to another and even more striking contradiction between what Rousseau says in the *Social Contract* and what he says elsewhere. Rousseau as he appears in the *Profession de foi* and indeed in most of his writings, published and unpublished, is clearly a Unitarian or Socinian, like Locke or Malebranche, regarding the minimal creed as a genuine, if not the

* *Lettres écrites de la montagne*, Letter 6, Pléiade, vol. 3, p. 807.
† *Political Writings*, ed. C. E. Vaughan, vol. 2, p. 445.
‡ *Profession de foi du vicaire savoyard*, ed. Beauvalon, Paris, 1937, pp. 134-5

only genuine, form of Christianity. Rousseau plainly detested the atheism of Diderot and the *philosophes*; his belief in the love of God and the life to come was profoundly important to him. He often said that he could not live without such religious faith. He also believed, much as Locke did, that such Christianity is reasonable.

In the *Social Contract*, however, his attitude is very much closer to that of Machiavelli than it is to that of Locke. What the state needs, Rousseau says in his chapter on the civil religion, is a religion subordinate to the state and designed to teach patriotic, civic and martial virtues. And Christianity, he says, quite as boldly as Machiavelli, is no good for this purpose; it teaches men to love the kingdom of heaven instead of their own republic on earth, and it teaches them to suffer but not to fight. It teaches the wrong virtues. Assuredly, Rousseau makes clear that he is talking here about civil religion, not private religion, and he admits that 'the religion of the Gospel' is the word of God for the private person. But the state religion is the more important, and the state religion must be supreme; Rousseau even goes so far as to propose a death penalty for those whose conduct is at variance with the religious principles they proclaim.

Up to a point Rousseau's argument is perfectly logical; he thinks that men will not become virtuous without the aid of religious institutions – a cult, a church – and since Christianity does not teach the civic virtue that is needed for the kind of republic he favours – a state on the model of Sparta or Rome – Rousseau is perfectly consistent in proposing, with Machiavelli, some kind of neo-pagan cult to match the needs of such a state. But how can he reconcile this with his professed faith in Christianity? Conceivably he is saying only that neo-paganism is useful and Gospel Christianity is true, and that the two belong to different logical categories, to be judged by different standards, the one by the standard of social utility and the other by that of truth; but if this is so, Rousseau is putting the useful above the true, and what then becomes of his criticism of his atheistic contemporaries, that they put utility in the place of morality?

An even more serious criticism of Rousseau can, I think, be levelled against his whole theory of liberty. On the one hand, he belongs to a certain tradition of moral philosophers who argue that to be free is not to be left to do what you want to do but to be enabled to do what you ought to do. Everything that Rousseau says about freedom being inseparable from justice, and about the necessary connexion between liberty and virtue, puts him in this school of morality. This theory of freedom, which has its origins in religious thought, claims to offer a superior, higher, more true and exalted analysis of what freedom is. Rousseau stands squarely in this tradition when he speaks of the higher, and more specifically moral freedom that men attain when they quit the state of nature and enter civil society.

But at the same time, Rousseau reveals an attachment to a less exalted idea of what freedom is. This is when he says that freedom is not being subject to any other *man*. Here one may suspect that Rousseau retained from the experiences of his life the simple notion – which might well be the occupational notion of domestic servants – that being dependent on another man is slavery and that freedom is simply having no master., To be dependent on things or institutions is quite different, and wholly unobjectionable. Throughout the *Social Contract* it is clear that Rousseau never sees institutions as a threat to freedom. The image of a King or Prince in Rousseau's eyes is the image of a master, and he sees such monarchs as enemies of liberty. But the image of the state touches him quite differently. There is a sentence in Book II (Chapter 12) of the *Social Contract* which illustrates this forcefully: this is where he says that things should be so arranged that every citizen is perfectly independent from all his fellow citizens and excessively dependent on the republic'. The word 'excessive' is significant. And why does Rousseau use it? Because he thinks such dependence can never be too great; because dependence on the state guarantees men against all dependence on men, against *'toute dépendance personnelle'*.

Is this a philosopher's concept of freedom? Perhaps; but is it not also like that of a footman? The dream of liberty in the servants' hall is the dream of the elimination of the master; translated into political terms, this becomes the republican fantasy that freedom lies in the elimination of the King. Of course Rousseau says a great deal more than this about freedom. He says that to be free means to live under a law of one's own enactment. But one does not have to progress very far through the pages of the *Social Contract* to see how modest this role of enactment is allowed to become. Men, he insists, are ignorant. The general will is morally sound, it is always rightful, but it is unenlightened. Men cannot be trusted to frame or devise their own laws. They need a Lawgiver to make laws for them. Their part in the enactment of laws is limited to *assent* to those laws. Thus freedom for Rousseau consists of putting oneself willingly under rules devised by someone else.

The measure of confidence that Rousseau has in his fellow men is made clear in *Émile*. At the very end of that long book, when the hero is grown up, and his exemplary education has produced its paragon, the young man, who is married and about to have a child, begs his tutor to stay with him: 'Advise and control us,' he implores the tutor, '. . . as long as I live I shall need you. I need you more than ever now that I am taking on the duties of manhood.'*

And just as the Tutor is the dominant figure of *Émile* so does the Lawgiver become the dominant figure of the *Social*

* *Émile*, ed. cit., p. 596.

42

Contract. Indeed the Lawgiver repeats in the state the role that the Tutor performs for the individual.* He is needed for the same reason; men left alone will be led by their own passions and folly into disaster; they need someone to save them from themselves.

It is a bad thing to have a master; for that is the reverse of freedom. But it is a good thing to have a tutor, so long as we follow him willingly and gladly. For Rousseau the way to liberty is the path of voluntary submission. 'The King is dead; long live the Lawgiver!' Is this, in the end, the battle cry of the republic? Does Rousseau wish us to say: 'Advise and control us, O *Législateur.* As long as we live we shall need you. We need you more than ever now that we are taking on the duties of self-government.'?

Many readers may find the *Social Contract* a frustrating book. What is offered with one hand is taken away with the other. It is theoretically possible for a political system to be so devised that men become more free by entering into it. This is to 'take laws as they might be'. On the other hand, it is hard, indeed impossible, to see how such a system could avoid being spoiled. This is to 'take men as they are'. Rousseau enlarges our vision and perhaps also our insight; at the same time he diminishes our expectations.

* See Judith N. Shklar, 'Rousseau's Images of Authority', *American Political Science Review*, December 1964, p. 919, and Pierre Burgelin, 'Le Social et Le Politique chez Rousseau' in *Journées d'Étude*, ed. cit., p. 173.

THE
SOCIAL CONTRACT

or

PRINCIPLES
OF
POLITICAL RIGHT

by

J.-J. Rousseau
CITIZEN OF GENEVA

– foederis aequas
Dicamus leges
AENEID, XI

FOREWORD

THIS little treatise is part of a larger work which I undertook many years ago without thinking of the limitations of my powers, and have long since abandoned. Of the various fragments that might have been taken from what I wrote, this is the most considerable, and the one I think the least unworthy of being offered to the public. The rest no longer exists.

BOOK I

My purpose is to consider if, in political society, there can be any legitimate and sure principle of government, taking men as they are and laws as they might be. In this inquiry I shall try always to bring together what right permits with what interest prescribes so that justice and utility are in no way divided.

I start without seeking to prove the importance of my subject. I may be asked whether I am a prince or a legislator that I should be writing about politics. I answer no: and indeed that that is my reason for doing so. If I were a prince or a legislator I should not waste my time saying what ought to be done; I should do it or keep silent.

Born as I was the citizen of a free state and a member of its sovereign body, the very right to vote imposes on me the duty to instruct myself in public affairs, however little influence my voice may have in them. And whenever I reflect upon governments, I am happy to find that my studies always give me fresh reasons for admiring that of my own country.

CHAPTER I

The subject of Book I

Man was born free, and he is everywhere in chains. Those who think themselves the masters of others are indeed greater slaves than they. How did this transformation come about? I do not know. How can it be made legitimate? That question I believe I can answer.

If I were to consider only force and the effects of force, I should say: 'So long as a people is constrained to obey, and obeys, it does well; but as soon as it can shake off the yoke, and shakes it off, it does better; for since it regains its freedom by the same right as that which removed it, a people is either justified in taking back its freedom, or there is no justifying those who took it away.' But the social order is a sacred right which serves as a basis for all other rights. And as it is not a natural right, it must be one founded on covenants. The problem is to determine what those covenants are. But before we pass on to that question, I must substantiate what I have so far said.

CHAPTER 2

The First Societies

THE oldest of all societies, and the only natural one, is that of the family; yet children remain tied to their father by nature only so long as they need him for their preservation. As soon as this need ends, the natural bond is dissolved. Once the children are freed from the obedience they owe their father, and the father is freed from his responsibilities towards them, both parties equally regain their independence. If they continue to remain united, it is no longer nature, but their own choice, which unites them; and the family as such is kept in being only by agreement.

This common liberty is a consequence of man's nature. Man's first law is to watch over his own preservation; his first care he owes to himself; and as soon as he reaches the age of reason, he becomes the only judge of the best means to preserve himself; he becomes his own master.

The family may therefore perhaps be seen as the first model of political societies: the head of the state bears the image of the father, the people the image of his children, and all, being born free and equal, surrender their freedom only when they see advantage in doing so. The only difference is that in the family, a father's love for his children repays him for the care he bestows on them, while in the state, where the ruler can have no such feeling for his people, the pleasure of commanding must take the place of love.

Grotius denies that all human government is established for the benefit of the governed, and he cites the example of slavery. His characteristic method of reasoning is always to offer fact as a proof of right.* It is possible to imagine a more logical method, but not one more favourable to tyrants.

According to Grotius, therefore, it is doubtful whether humanity belongs to a hundred men, or whether these hundred men belong to humanity, though he seems throughout his book to lean to the first of these views, which is also that of Hobbes. These authors show us the human race divided into herds of cattle, each with a master who preserves it only in order to devour its members.

Just as a shepherd possesses a nature superior to that of his flock, so do those shepherds of men, their rulers, have a nature superior to that of their people. Or so, we are told by Philo, the Emperor Caligula argued, concluding, reasonably enough on this same analogy, that kings were gods or alternatively that the people were animals.

The reasoning of Caligula coincides with that of Hobbes and Grotius. Indeed Aristotle, before any of them, said that men were not at all equal by nature, since some were born for slavery and others born to be masters.

Aristotle was right; but he mistook the effect for the cause. Anyone born in slavery is born for slavery – nothing is more

* 'Learned researches on public law are often only the history of ancient abuses, and one is misled when one gives oneself the trouble of studying them too closely.' *Traité manuscrit des intérêts de la France avec ses voisins* par M. L. M. d'A. This is exactly what Grotius does. [Rousseau's quotation is from the Marquis d'Argenson. *Trans.*]

certain. Slaves, in their bondage, lose everything, even the desire to be free. They love their servitude even as the companions of Ulysses loved their life as brutes.* But if there are slaves by nature, it is only because there has been slavery against nature. Force made the first slaves; and their cowardice perpetuates their slavery.

I have said nothing of the King Adam or of the Emperor Noah, father of the three great monarchs who shared out the universe among them, like the children of Saturn, with whom some authors have identified them. I hope my readers will be grateful for this moderation, for since I am directly descended from one of those princes, and perhaps in the eldest line, how do I know that if the deeds were checked, I might not find myself the legitimate king of the human race? However that may be, there is no gainsaying that Adam was the king of the world, as was Robinson Crusoe of his island, precisely because he was the sole inhabitant; and the great advantage of such an empire was that the monarch, secure upon his throne, had no occasion to fear rebellions, wars or conspirators.

CHAPTER 3

The Right of the Strongest

THE strongest man is never strong enough to be master all the time, unless he transforms force into right and obedience into duty. Hence 'the right of the strongest' – a 'right' that sounds like something intended ironically, but is actually laid down as a principle. But shall we never have this phrase explained? Force is a physical power; I do not see how its effects could produce morality. To yield to force is an act of necessity, not of will; it is at best an act of prudence. In what sense can it be a moral duty?

* See a short treatise of Plutarch entitled: *That Animals use Reason.*

Let us grant, for a moment, that this so-called right exists. I suggest it can only produce a tissue of bewildering nonsense; for once might is made to be right, cause and effect are reversed, and every force which overcomes another force inherits the right which belonged to the vanquished. As soon as man can disobey with impunity, his disobedience becomes legitimate; and as the strongest is always right, the only problem is how to become the strongest. But what can be the validity of a right which perishes with the force on which it rests? If force compels obedience, there is no need to invoke a duty to obey, and if force ceases to compel obedience, there is no longer any obligation. Thus the word 'right' adds nothing to what is said by 'force'; it is meaningless.

'Obey those in power.' If this means 'yield to force' the precept is sound, but superfluous; it has never, I suggest, been violated. All power comes from God, I agree; but so does every disease, and no one forbids us to summon a physician. If I am held up by a robber at the edge of a wood, force compels me to hand over my purse. But if I could somehow contrive to keep the purse from him, would I still be obliged in conscience to surrender it? After all, the pistol in the robber's hand is undoubtedly a *power*.

Surely it must be admitted, then, that might does not make right, and that the duty of obedience is owed only to legitimate powers. Thus we are constantly led back to my original question.

CHAPTER 4

Slavery

SINCE no man has any natural authority over his fellows, and since force alone bestows no right, all legitimate authority among men must be based on covenants.

Grotius says: 'If an individual can alienate his freedom and become the slave of a master, why may not a whole people alienate its freedom and become the subject of a king?' In this remark there are several ambiguous words which call for explanation; but let us confine ourselves to one – to 'alienate'. To alienate is to give or sell. A man who becomes the slave of another does not give himself, he sells himself in return for at least a subsistence. But in return for what could a whole people be said to sell itself? A king, far from nourishing his subjects, draws his nourishment from them; and kings, according to Rabelais, need more than a little nourishment. Do subjects, then, give their persons to the king on condition that he will accept their property as well? If so, I fail to see what they have left to preserve.

It will be said that a despot gives his subjects the assurance of civil tranquillity. Very well, but what does it profit them, if those wars against other powers which result from a despot's ambition, if his insatiable greed, and the oppressive demands of his administration, cause more desolation than civil strife would cause? What do the people gain if their very condition of civil tranquillity is one of their hardships? There is peace in dungeons, but is that enough to make dungeons desirable? The Greeks lived in peace in the cave of Cyclops awaiting their turn to be devoured.

To speak of a man giving himself in return for nothing is to speak of what is absurd, unthinkable; such an action would be illegitimate, void, if only because no one who did it could be in his right mind. To say the same of a whole people is to conjure up a nation of lunatics; and right cannot rest on madness.

Even if each individual could alienate himself, he cannot alienate his children. For they are born men; they are born free; their liberty belongs to them; no one but they themselves has the right to dispose of it. Before they reach the years of discretion, their father may, in their name, make certain rules for their protection and their welfare, but he cannot give away their liberty irrevocably and unconditionally, for such a gift would be contrary to the natural order and an abuse of paternal right. Hence, an arbitrary government would be legitimate only if every new generation were free to accept or reject it, and in that case the government would cease to be arbitrary.

To renounce freedom is to renounce one's humanity, one's rights as a man and equally one's duties. There is no possible *quid pro quo* for one who renounces everything; indeed such renunciation is contrary to man's very nature; for if you take away all freedom of the will, you strip a man's actions of all moral significance. Finally, any covenant which stipulated absolute dominion for one party and absolute obedience for the other would be illogical and nugatory. Is it not evident that he who is entitled to demand everything owes nothing? And does not the single fact of there being no reciprocity, no mutual obligation, nullify the act? For what right can my slave have against me? If everything he has belongs to me, his right is *my* right, and it would be nonsense to speak of my having a right *against* myself.

Grotius and the rest claim to find in war another justification for the so-called right of slavery. They argue that the victor's having the right to kill the vanquished implies that the vanquished has the right to purchase his life at the expense of his liberty – a bargain thought to be the more legitimate because it is advantageous to both parties.

But it is clear that this so-called right to kill the vanquished cannot be derived from the state of war. For this reason alone, that men living in their primitive condition of independence have no intercourse regular enough to constitute either a state of peace or a state of war; and men are not naturally enemies. It is conflicts over things, not quarrels between men which constitute war, and the state of war cannot arise from mere personal relations, but only from property relations. Private wars between one man and another can exist neither in a state of nature, where there is no fixed property, nor in society, where everything is under the authority of law.

Private fights, duels, encounters, do not constitute any kind of state; and as for the private wars that were permitted by the ordinances of Louis IX, King of France, and suspended by the Peace of God, these were no more than an abuse of feudal government, an irrational system if there ever was one, and contrary both to natural justice and to all sound polity.

War, then, is not a relation between men, but between states; in war individuals are enemies wholly by chance, not as men, not even as citizens,* but only as soldiers; not as members of their country, but only as its defenders. In a word, a state can have as an enemy only another state, not men, because there can be no real relation between things possessing different intrinsic natures.

This principle conforms to the established rules of all times and to the constant practice of every political society. Declarations of war are warnings not so much to governments as to their subjects. The foreigner – whether he is a king, a private person or a whole people – who robs, kills or detains the

* The Romans, who understood and respected the rights of war better than any other nation, carried their scruples on this subject so far that a citizen was forbidden to volunteer without engaging himself expressly against the enemy and against an enemy specifically named. When the legion in which the younger Cato fought his first campaign under Popilius was re-formed, the elder Cato wrote to Popilius saying that if he wished his son to continue to serve under him, he should administer a fresh military oath, on the grounds that his son's first oath was annulled, and that he could no longer bear arms against the enemy. Cato also wrote to his son warning him not to go into battle without first taking the oath.

I realize that the siege of Clusium and other incidents from Roman history may be quoted against me, but I am citing laws and customs. No nation has broken its own laws less frequently than the Romans, and no nation has ever had such excellent laws. [Footnote added in the Edition of 1782.]

subjects of another prince without first declaring war against that prince, is not an enemy but a brigand. Even in the midst of war, a just prince, seizing what he can of public property in the enemy's territory, nevertheless respects the persons and possessions of private individuals; he respects the principles on which his own rights are based. Since the aim of war is to subdue a hostile state, a combatant has the right to kill the defenders of that state while they are armed; but as soon as they lay down their arms and surrender, they cease to be either enemies or instruments of the enemy; they become simply men once more, and no one has any longer the right to take their lives. It is sometimes possible to destroy a state without killing a single one of its members, and war gives no right to inflict any more destruction than is necessary for victory. These principles were not invented by Grotius, nor are they founded on the authority of the poets; they are derived from the nature of things; they are based on reason.

The right of conquest has no other foundation than the law of the strongest. And if war gives the conqueror no right to massacre a conquered people, no such right can be invoked to justify their enslavement. Men have the right to kill their enemies only when they cannot enslave them, so the right of enslaving cannot be derived from the right to kill. It would therefore be an iniquitous barter to make the vanquished purchase with their liberty the lives over which the victor has no legitimate claim. An argument basing the right over life and death on the right to enslave, and the right to enslave on the right over life and death, is an argument trapped in a vicious circle.

Even if we assumed that this terrible right of massacre did exist, then slaves of war, or a conquered people, would be under no obligation to obey their master any further than they were forced to do so. By taking an equivalent of his victim's life, the victor shows him no favour; instead of destroying him unprofitably, he destroys him by exploiting him. Hence, far from the victor having acquired some further authority beside that of force over the vanquished, the state of war between them continues; their mutual relation is the effect of war, and the continuation of the rights of war implies that there has been no treaty of peace. An agreement has assuredly been made, but that agreement, far from ending the state of war, presupposes its continuation.

Thus, however we look at the question, the 'right' of slavery is seen to be void; void, not only because it cannot be justified, but also because it is nonsensical, because it has no meaning. The words 'slavery' and 'right' are contradictory, they cancel each other out. Whether as between one man and another, or between one man and a whole people, it would always be absurd to say: 'I hereby make a covenant with you which is wholly at your expense and wholly to my advantage; I will respect it so long as I please and you shall respect it so long as I wish.'

CHAPTER 5

That We Must Always Go Back To an Original Covenant

EVEN if I were to concede all that I have so far refuted, the champions of despotism would be no better off. There will always be a great difference between subduing a multitude and ruling a society. If one man successively enslaved many separate individuals, no matter how numerous, he and they would never bear the aspect of anything but a master and his slaves, not at all that of a people and their ruler; an aggregation, perhaps, but certainly not an association, for they would neither have a common good nor be a body politic. Even if such a man were to enslave half the world, he would remain a private individual, and his interest, always at variance with that of the others, would never be more than a personal interest. When he died, the empire he left would be scattered for lack of any bond of union, even as an oak crumbles and falls into a heap of ashes when fire has consumed it.

'A people,' says Grotius, 'may give itself to a king.' Therefore, according to Grotius a people is *a people* even before the gift to the king is made. The gift itself is a civil act; it presupposes public deliberation. Hence, before considering the act by which a people submits to a king, we ought to scrutinize the act by which people become *a* people, for that act, being necessarily antecedent to the other, is the real foundation of society.

Indeed, if there were no earlier agreement, then how, unless the election were unanimous, could there be any obligation on the minority to accept the decision of the majority? What right have the hundred who want to have a master to vote on behalf of the ten who do not? The law of majority-voting itself rests on a covenant, and implies that there has been on at least one occasion unanimity.

CHAPTER 6

The Social Pact

I ASSUME that men reach a point where the obstacles to their preservation in a state of nature prove greater than the strength that each man has to preserve himself in that state. Beyond this point, the primitive condition cannot endure, for then the human race will perish if it does not change its mode of existence.

Since men cannot create new forces, but merely combine and control those which already exist, the only way in which they can preserve themselves is by uniting their separate powers in a combination strong enough to overcome any resistance, uniting them so that their powers are directed by a single motive and act in concert.

Such a sum of forces can be produced only by the union of separate men, but as each man's own strength and liberty are the chief instruments of his preservation, how can he merge his with others' without putting himself in peril and neglecting the care he owes to himself? This difficulty, which brings me back to my present subject, may be expressed in these words:

'How to find a form of association which will defend the person and goods of each member with the collective force of all, and under which each individual, while uniting himself with the others, obeys no one but himself, and remains as free as before.' This is the fundamental problem to which the social contract holds the solution.

The articles of this contract are so precisely determined by the nature of the act, that the slightest modification must render them null and void; they are such that, though perhaps never formally stated, they are everywhere the same, everywhere tacitly admitted and recognized; and if ever the social pact is violated, every man regains his original rights and, recovering his natural freedom, loses that social freedom for which he exchanged it.

These articles of association, rightly understood, are reducible to a single one, namely the total alienation by each associate of himself and all his rights to the whole community. Thus, in the first place, as every individual gives himself absolutely, the conditions are the same for all, and precisely because they are the same for all, it is in no one's interest to make the conditions onerous for others.

Secondly, since the alienation is unconditional, the union is as perfect as it could be, and no individual associate has any longer any rights to claim; for if rights were left to individuals, in the absence of any higher authority to judge between them and the public, each individual, being his own judge in some causes, would soon demand to be his own judge in all; and in this way the state of nature would be kept in being, and the association inevitably become either tyrannical or void.

Finally, since each man gives himself to all, he gives himself to no one; and since there is no associate over whom he does not gain the same rights as others gain over him, each man recovers the equivalent of everything he loses, and in the bargain he acquires more power to preserve what he has.

If, then, we eliminate from the social pact everything that is not essential to it, we find it comes down to this: 'Each one of us puts into the community his person and all his powers under the supreme direction of the general will; and as a body, we incorporate every member as an indivisible part of the whole.'

Immediately, in place of the individual person of each contracting party, this act of association creates an artificial and collective body composed of as many members as there are voters in the assembly, and by this same act that body acquires its unity, its common *ego*, its life and its will. The public person thus formed by the union of all other persons was once called the *city*,* and is now known as the *republic* or the *body politic*. In its passive role it is called the *state*, when it

---

* The real meaning of this word has been almost entirely lost in the modern world, when a town and a city are thought to be identical, and a citizen the same as a burgess. People forget that houses may make a town, while only citizens can make a city. The Carthaginians once paid dearly for this mistake. I have never read of the title *cives* being given to the subject of any prince, not even to the Macedonians in ancient times or the English today, in spite of their being closer to liberty than any other people. The French alone apply the name 'Citizen' freely to everyone, and that is because they do not know what it means, as their Dictionaries prove; if they did know, they would be guilty, in usurping it, of *lèse-majesté*; as it is, they use the word to designate social status and not legal right. When Bodin wanted to speak of citizens and burgesses, he made the gross error of mistaking the one for the other. Monsieur d'Alembert avoids this mistake; and in his article on 'Geneva' he correctly distinguishes between the four orders of men (five, if aliens are included) which are found in our town, and of which only two compose the republic. No other French author to my knowledge has understood the real meaning of the word 'citizen'.

plays an active role it is the *sovereign*; and when it is compared to others of its own kind, it is a *power*. Those who are associated in it take collectively the name of *a people*, and call themselves individually *citizens*, in so far as they share in the sovereign power, and *subjects*, in so far as they put themselves under the laws of the state. However, these words are often confused, each being mistaken for another; but the essential thing is to know how to recognize them when they are used in their precise sense.

CHAPTER 7

The Sovereign

THIS formula shows that the act of association consists of a reciprocal commitment between society and the individual, so that each person, in making a contract, as it were, with himself, finds himself doubly committed, first, as a member of the sovereign body in relation to individuals, and secondly as a member of the state in relation to the sovereign. Here there can be no invoking the principle of civil law which says that no man is bound by a contract with himself, for there is a great difference between having an obligation to oneself and having an obligation to something of which one is a member.

We must add that a public decision can impose an obligation on all the subjects towards the sovereign, by reason of the two aspects under which each can be seen, while, contrariwise, such decisions cannot impose an obligation on the sovereign towards itself; and hence it would be against the very nature of a political body for the sovereign to set over itself a law which it could not infringe. The sovereign, bearing only one single and identical aspect, is in the position of a private person making a contract with himself, which shows that there neither is, nor can be, any kind of fundamental law binding on the people as a body, not even the social contract itself. This does not mean that the whole body cannot incur obligations to other nations, so long as those obligations do not infringe the contract; for in relation to foreign powers, the body politic is a simple entity, an individual.

However, since the body politic, or sovereign, owes its being to the sanctity of the contract alone, it cannot commit itself, even in treaties with foreign powers, to anything that would derogate from the original act of association; it could not, for example, alienate a part of itself or submit to another sovereign. To violate the act which has given it existence would be to annihilate itself; and what is nothing can produce nothing.

As soon as the multitude is united thus in a single body, no one can injure any one of the members without attacking the whole, still less injure the whole without each member feeling it. Duty and self-interest thus equally oblige the two contracting parties to give each other mutual aid; and the same men should seek to bring together in this dual relationship, all the advantages that flow from it.

Now, as the sovereign is formed entirely of the individuals who compose it, it has not, nor could it have, any interest contrary to theirs; and so the sovereign has no need to give guarantees to the subjects, because it is impossible for a body to wish to hurt all of its members, and, as we shall see, it cannot hurt any particular member. The sovereign by the mere fact that it is, is always all that it ought to be.

But this is not true of the relation of subject to sovereign. Despite their common interest, subjects will not be bound by their commitment unless means are found to guarantee their fidelity.

For every individual as a man may have a private will contrary to, or different from, the general will that he has as a citizen. His private interest may speak with a very different voice from that of the public interest; his absolute and naturally independent existence may make him regard what he owes to the common cause as a gratuitous contribution, the loss of which would be less painful for others than the payment is onerous for him; and fancying that the artificial person which constitutes the state is a mere rational entity (since it is not a man), he might seek to enjoy the rights of a citizen without doing the duties of a subject. The growth of this kind of injustice would bring about the ruin of the body politic.

Hence, in order that the social pact shall not be an empty formula, it is tacitly implied in that commitment – which alone can give force to all others – that whoever refuses to obey the general will shall be constrained to do so by the whole body, which means nothing other than that he shall be forced to be free; for this is the condition which, by giving each citizen to the nation, secures him against all personal dependence, it is the condition which shapes both the design and the working of the political machine, and which alone bestows justice on civil contracts – without it, such contracts would be absurd, tyrannical and liable to the grossest abuse.

CHAPTER 8

Civil Society

THE passing from the state of nature to the civil society produces a remarkable change in man; it puts justice as a rule of conduct in the place of instinct, and gives his actions the moral quality they previously lacked. It is only then, when the voice of duty has taken the place of physical impulse, and right that of desire, that man, who has hitherto thought only of himself, finds himself compelled to act on other principles, and to consult his reason rather than study his inclinations. And although in civil society man surrenders some of the advantages that belong to the state of nature, he gains in return far greater ones; his faculties are so exercised and developed, his mind is so enlarged, his sentiments so ennobled, and his whole spirit so elevated that, if the abuse of his new condition did not in many cases lower him to something worse than what he had left, he should constantly bless the happy hour that lifted him for ever from the state of nature and from a narrow, stupid animal made a creature of intelligence and a man.

Suppose we draw up a balance sheet, so that the losses and gains may be readily compared. What man loses by the social contract is his natural liberty and the absolute right to anything that tempts him and that he can take; what he gains by the social contract is civil liberty and the legal right of property in what he possesses. If we are to avoid mistakes in weighing the one side against the other, we must clearly distinguish between *natural* liberty, which has no limit but the physical power of the individual concerned, and *civil* liberty, which is limited by the general will; and we must distinguish also between *possession*, which is based only on force or 'the right of the first occupant', and *property*, which must rest on a legal title.

We might also add that man acquires with civil society, moral freedom, which alone makes man the master of himself; for to be governed by appetite alone is slavery, while obedience to a law one prescribes to oneself is freedom. However, I have already said more than enough on this subject, and the philosophical meaning of the word 'freedom' is no part of my subject here.

CHAPTER 9

Of Estate

EVERY member of the community gives himself to it at the moment it is brought into being just as he is – he himself, with all his resources, including all his goods. This is not to say that possession by this act changes its nature in changing hands and becomes property in the grasp of the sovereign; but rather, that as the resources of the nation are incomparably greater than those of an individual, public possession is in simple fact more secure and more irrevocable than private possession, without being any more legitimate – at any rate, in the eyes of foreigners; for the state, *vis-à-vis* its own members, becomes master of all their goods by virtue of the social contract, which serves, within the state, as the basis of all other rights; while *vis-à-vis* other nations, the state has only the 'right of the first occupant', which it derives from individuals.

The 'right of the first occupant', although more real than the 'right of the strongest', does not become a true right until the institution of property. Every man has a natural right to what he needs; but the positive act which makes a man the proprietor of any estate excludes him from everything else. His share having once been settled, he must confine himself to it, and he has no further right against the community. Thus we see how 'the right of the first occupant', weak as it is in the state of nature, compels in political society the respect of all men. What this right makes one aware of is less what belongs to others than what does *not* belong to oneself.

As a general rule, to justify the right of the first occupant to any piece of land whatever, the following conditions must obtain: first, that the land shall not already be inhabited by anyone else; secondly, that the claimant occupies no more than he needs for subsistence; thirdly, that he takes possession, not by an idle ceremony, but by actually working and cultivating the soil – the only sign of ownership which need be respected by other people in the absence of a legal title.

It can, indeed, be said that tying 'the right of the first occupant' to need and work is stretching it as far as it will go. Can one really avoid setting limits on the right? Is it enough to put one's feet on a piece of common land in order to claim it at once as one's own? Is it enough to have the power to keep other men off for one moment in order to deprive them of the right ever to return? How could a man or a people seize a vast territory and keep out the rest of the human race except by a criminal usurpation – since the action would rob the rest of mankind of the shelter and the food that nature has given them all in common? When Nunez Balbao stood on the shore and took possession of the southern seas and of South America in the name of the crown of Castille, was that enough to dispossess all the inhabitants and to exclude all the other princes of the world? If so, such idle ceremonies would have had no end; and the Catholic King might without leaving his royal chamber have taken possession of the whole universe, only excepting afterwards those parts of his empire already belonging to other princes.

We can see how the lands of private persons, when they are united and contiguous, become public territory; and how the right of sovereignty, extending from the subjects to the soil they occupy, covers both property and persons; it makes the owners all the more dependent, and turns their own strength into the guarantee of their fidelity. This advantage seems to have eluded the ancient monarchs, who, in calling themselves simply the King of the Persians or the Scythians or the Macedonians, appear to have regarded themselves rather as rulers of men than as masters of their countries. Monarchs of the present day call themselves more shrewdly the King of France, or of Spain, or of England and so on; in holding thus the land, they are very sure of holding the inhabitants.

What is unique about the alienation entailed by the social contract is that the community in accepting the goods of an individual is far from depriving him of them; on the contrary it simply assures him of their lawful possession; it changes usurpation into valid right and mere enjoyment into legal ownership. Since every owner is regarded as a trustee of the public property, his rights are respected by every other member of the state, and protected with its collective force against foreigners; men have, by a surrender which is advantageous to the public and still more to themselves, acquired, so to speak, all that they have given up – a paradox which is easily explained by the distinction between the rights which the soverign has and which the owner has over the same property, as will be seen later.

It may also happen that men begin to unite before they possess anything, and spreading over a territory large enough for them all, proceed to enjoy it in common, or, alternatively, divide it among themselves either equally or in shares determined by the sovereign. In whatever manner this acquisition is made, the right of any individual over his own estate is always subordinate to the right of the community over everything; for without this there would be neither strength in the social bond nor effective force in the exercise of sovereignty.

I shall end this chapter – and Book I – with an observation which might serve as a basis for the whole social system: namely, that the social pact, far from destroying natural equality, substitutes, on the contrary, a moral and lawful equality for whatever physical inequality that nature may have imposed on mankind; so that however unequal in strength and intelligence, men become equal by covenant and by right.*

---

* Under a bad government, this equality is only an appearance and an illusion; it serves only to keep the poor in their wretchedness and sustain the rich in their usurpation. In truth, laws are always useful to those with possessions and harmful to those who have nothing; from which it follows that the social state is advantageous to men only when all possess something and none has too much.

BOOK II

CHAPTER I

That Sovereignty is Inalienable

THE first and most important consequence of the principles so far established is that the general will alone can direct the forces of the state in accordance with that end which the state has been established to achieve – the common good; for if conflict between private interests has made the setting up of civil societies necessary, harmony between those same interests has made it possible. It is what is common to those different interests which yields the social bond; if there were no point on which separate interests coincided, then society could not conceivably exist. And it is precisely on the basis of this common interest that society must be governed.

My argument, then, is that sovereignty, being nothing other than the exercise of the general will, can never be alienated; and that the sovereign, which is simply a collective being, cannot be represented by anyone but itself – power may be delegated, but the will cannot be.

For indeed while it is not impossible for a private will to coincide with the general will on some point or other, it is impossible for such a coincidence to be regular and enduring; for the private will inclines by its very nature towards partiality, and the general will towards equality. It is even more inconceivable that there should be a guarantee of harmony between the private and the general will, even if it were to continue always, for such lasting harmony would be the result of chance and not of design. The sovereign could say: 'What I want at present is precisely what this man wants, or at least what he says he wants'; but no sovereign could say:

'What this man is going to want tomorrow I too shall want', for it is absurd that anyone should wish to bind himself for the future, and it is a contradiction in terms to say that any human being should wish to consent to something that is the reverse of his own good. If a people promises simply and solely to obey, it dissolves itself by that very pledge; it ceases to be a people; for once there is a master, there is no longer a sovereign, and the body politic is therefore annihilated.

This is not to say that the commands of leaders may not pass for the general will if the sovereign, being free to oppose them, does not do so. In such a case the silence of the people permits the assumption that the people consents. This will be explained more fully in a later chapter.

CHAPTER 2

That Sovereignty is Indivisible

JUST as sovereignty is inalienable, it is for the same reason indivisible; for either the will is general* or it is not; either it is the will of the body of the people, or merely that of a part. In the first case, a declaration of will is an act of sovereignty and constitutes law; in the second case, it is only a declaration of a particular will or an act of administration, it is at best a mere decree.

Nevertheless, our political theorists, unable to divide the principle of sovereignty, divide it in its purpose; they divide it into power and will, divide it, that is, into executive and legislative, into the rights of levying taxation, administering justice and making war, into domestic jurisdiction and the power to deal with foreign governments. Sometimes our theorists confuse all the parts and sometimes they separate

---

* For the will to be general, it does not always have to be unanimous; but all the votes must be counted. Any formal exclusion destroys its universality.

them. They make the sovereign a creature of fantasy, a patch-work of separate pieces, rather as if they were to construct a man of several bodies – one with eyes, one with legs, the other with feet and nothing else. It is said that Japanese mountebanks can cut up a child under the eyes of spectators, throw the different parts into the air, and then make the child come down, alive and all of a piece. This is more or less the trick that our political theorists perform – after dismembering the social body with a sleight of hand worthy of the fairground, they put the pieces together again anyhow.

The mistake comes from having no precise notion of what sovereign authority is, and from taking mere manifestations of authority for parts of the authority itself. For instance, the acts of declaring war and making peace have been regarded as acts of sovereignty, which they are not; for neither of these acts constitutes a *law*, but only an application of law, a particular act which determines how the law shall be interpreted – and all this will be obvious as soon as I have defined the idea which attaches to the word 'law'.

If we were to scrutinize in the same way the other supposed divisions of sovereignty, we should find that whenever we thought that sovereignty was divided, we had been mistaken, for the rights which are taken to be part of that sovereignty prove in fact to be subordinate to it, and presuppose the existence of a supreme will which they merely serve to put into effect.

This want of precision has obfuscated immeasurably the conclusions of our legal theorists when they have come to apply their own principles to determine the respective rights of kings and of peoples. Every reader of the third and fourth chapters of the first Book of Grotius can see how that learned man and his translator, Barbeyrac, are trapped in their own sophisms, frightened of saying either too much or alter-natively too little (according to their prejudices) and so offending the interests they wish to flatter. Grotius, a refugee in France, discontented with his own country and out to pay court to Louis XIII, to whom his book is dedicated, spares no pains to rob peoples of all their rights and to invest those rights, by every conceivable artifice, in kings. This would have been very much to the taste of Barbeyrac, who dedicated his translation of Grotius to the King of England, George I. But unfortunately the expulsion of James II – which Barbeyrac calls an 'abdication' – obliged him to speak with a marked reserve, to hesitate and equivocate, so as not to suggest that William III was a usurper. If these two writers had adopted sound principles, all their difficulties would have vanished, and their arguments would have been logical; but then they would, alas for them, have told the truth and paid court only to the people. The truth brings no man a fortune; and it is not the people who hand out embassies, professorships and pensions.

CHAPTER 3

Whether the General Will Can Err

IT follows from what I have argued that the general will is always rightful and always tends to the public good; but it does not follow that the decisions of the people are always equally right. We always want what is advantageous but we do not always discern it. The people is never corrupted, but it is often misled; and only then does it seem to will what is bad.

There is often a great difference between the will of all [what all individuals want] and the general will; the general will studies only the common interest while the will of all studies private interest, and is indeed no more than the sum of individual desires. But if we take away from these same wills, the pluses and minuses which cancel each other out, the sum of the difference is the general will.*

From the deliberations of a people properly informed, and provided its members do not have any communication among themselves, the great number of small differences will always produce a general will and the decision will always be good. But if groups, sectional associations are formed at the expense of the larger association, the will of each of these groups will become general in relation to its own members and private in relation to the state; we might then say that there are no longer as many votes as there are men but only as many votes as there are groups. The differences become less numerous and yield a result less general. Finally, when one of these groups becomes so large that it can dominate the rest, the result is no longer the sum of many small differences, but one great divisive difference; then there ceases to be a general will, and the opinion which prevails is no more than a private opinion.

Thus if the general will is to be clearly expressed, it is imperative that there should be no sectional associations in the state, and that every citizen should make up his own mind for himself † – such was the unique and sublime invention of the great Lycurgus. But if there are sectional associations, it is wise to multiply their number and to prevent inequality

* 'Every interest,' says the Marquis d'Argenson, 'has its different principles. Harmony between two interests is created by opposition to that of a third.' He might have added that the harmony of all interests is created by opposition to those of each. If there were no different interests, we should hardly be conscious of a common interest, as there would be no resistance to it; everything would run easily of its own accord, and politics would cease to be an art.

† 'Divisions,' says Machiavelli, 'sometimes injure and sometimes aid a republic. The injury is done by cabals and factions; the service is rendered by a party which maintains itself without cabals and factions. Since, therefore, it is impossible for the founder of a republic to provide against enmities, he must make the best provision he can against factions.' *History of Florence*, Book VII. [Original in Italian. *Trans.*]

among them, as Solon, Numa and Servius did. These are the only precautions which can ensure that the general will is always enlightened and the people protected from error.

CHAPTER 4

The Limits of Sovereign Power

IF the state, or the nation, is nothing other than a legal person the life of which consists in the union of its members and if the most important of its cares is its own preservation, it must have a universal and compelling power to move and dispose of each part in whatever manner is beneficial to the whole. Just as nature gives each man an absolute power over all his own limbs, the social pact gives the body politic an absolute power over all its members; and it is this same power which, directed by the general will, bears, as I have said, the name of sovereignty.

However, we have to consider beside the public person those private persons who compose it, and whose life and liberty is naturally independent of it. Here we have to distinguish clearly the respective rights of the citizen and of the sovereign,* and distinguish those duties which the citizens have as subjects from the natural rights which they ought to enjoy as men.

We have agreed that each man alienates by the social pact only that part of his power, his goods and his liberty which is the concern of the community; but it must also be admitted that the sovereign alone is judge of what is of such concern.

Whatever services the citizen can render the state, he owes

* Please, attentive reader, do not hasten to accuse me of contradiction. I cannot avoid a contradiction of words, because of the poverty of language; but wait.

whenever the sovereign demands them; but the sovereign, on its side, may not impose on the subjects any burden which is not necessary to the community; the sovereign cannot, indeed, even will such a thing, since according to the law of reason no less than to the law of nature nothing is without a cause.

The commitments which bind us to the social body are obligatory only because they are mutual; and their nature is such that in fulfilling them a man cannot work for others without at the same time working for himself. How should it be that the general will is always rightful and that all men constantly wish the happiness of each but for the fact that there is no one who does not take that word 'each' to pertain to himself and in voting for all think of himself? This proves that the equality of rights and the notion of justice which it produces derive from the predilection which each man has for himself and hence from human nature as such. It also proves that the general will, to be truly what it is, must be general in its purpose as well as in its nature; that it should spring from all and apply to all; and that it loses its natural rectitude when it is directed towards any particular and circumscribed object – for in judging what is foreign to us, we have no sound principle of equity to guide us.

For, indeed, whenever we are dealing with a particular fact or right, on a matter which has not been settled by an earlier and general agreement, that question becomes contentious. It is a conflict in which private interests are ranged on one side and the public interest on the other; and I can see neither the law which is to be followed nor the judge who is to arbitrate. It would be absurd in such a dispute to seek an express decision of the general will; for a decision could only be a conclusion in favour of one of the contending parties, and it would be regarded by the other party as an alien, partial will, a will prone to error and liable in such circumstances to fall into injustice. So we see that even as a private will cannot represent the general will, so too the general will changes its nature if it seeks to deal with an individual case; it cannot as a *general* will give a ruling concerning any one man or any one fact. When the people of Athens, for example, appointed or dismissed its leaders, awarding honours to one, inflicting penalties on another, and by a multitude of particular decrees indiscriminately exercised all the functions of an administration, then the people of Athens no longer had what is correctly understood as a general will and ceased to act as sovereign and acted instead as magistrate. All this may seem at variance with commonly accepted notions; but I must be given time to expound my own.

It should nevertheless be clear from what I have so far said that the general will derives its generality less from the number of voices than from the common interest which unites them – for the general will is an institution in which each necessarily submits himself to the same conditions which he imposes on others; this admirable harmony of interest and justice gives to social deliberations a quality of equity which disappears at once from the discussion of any individual dispute precisely because in these latter cases there is no common interest to unite and identify the decision of the judge with that of the contending parties.

Whichever way we look at it, we always return to the same conclusion: namely that the social pact establishes equality among the citizens in that they all pledge themselves under the same conditions and must all enjoy the same rights. Hence by the nature of the compact, every act of sovereignty, that is, every authentic act of the general will, binds or favours all the citizens equally, so that the sovereign recognizes only the whole body of the nation and makes no distinction between any of the members who compose it. What then is correctly to be called an act of sovereignty? It is not a covenant between a superior and an inferior, but a covenant of the body with each of its members. It is a legitimate covenant, because its basis is the social contract; an equitable one, because it is common to all; a useful one, because it can have no end but the common good; and it is a durable covenant because it is guaranteed by the armed forces and the supreme power. So long as the subjects submit to such covenants alone, they obey nobody but their own will; and to ask how far the respective rights of the sovereign and the citizen extend is to ask how far these two can pledge themselves together, each to all and all to each.

From this it is clear that the sovereign power, wholly absolute, wholly sacred, wholly inviolable as it is, does not go beyond and cannot go beyond the limits of the general covenants; and thus that every man can do what he pleases with such goods and such freedom as is left to him by these covenants; and from this it follows that the sovereign has never any right to impose greater burdens on one subject than on another, for whenever that happens a private grievance is created and the sovereign's power is no longer competent.

Granted these distinctions, it becomes manifestly false to assert that individuals make any real renunciation by the social contract; indeed, as a result of the contract they find themselves in a situation preferable in real terms to that which prevailed before; instead of an alienation, they have profitably exchanged an uncertain and precarious life for a better and more secure one; they have exchanged natural independence for freedom, the power to destroy others for the enjoyment of their own security; they have exchanged their own strength which others might overcome for a right which the social union makes invincible. Their very lives, which they have pledged to the state, are always protected by it; and even when they risk their lives to defend the state, what more are they doing but giving back what they have received from the state? What are they doing that they would not do more often, and at greater peril, in the state of nature, where every man is inevitably at war and at the risk of his life, defends whatever serves him to maintain life? Assuredly, all must now fight in case of need for their country, but at least no one has any longer to fight for himself. And is there not something to be gained by running, for the sake of the guarantee of safety, a few of those risks we should each have to face alone if we were deprived of that assurance?

CHAPTER 5

The Right of Life and Death

IT will be asked how individuals, who have no right whatever to take their own lives, can transfer to the sovereign a right they do not possess. This question looks difficult to answer only because it is badly formulated. Every man has the right to risk his own life in order to preserve it. Has it ever been said that a man who leaps out of a window to escape from a fire is guilty of suicide? Would the same crime be imputed to a man who perishes in a storm on the grounds that he knew of the danger when he embarked?

The purpose of the social treaty is the preservation of the contracting parties. Whoever wills the end wills also the means, and certain risks, even certain casualties are inseparable from these means. Whoever wishes to preserve his own life at the expense of others must give his life for them when it is necessary. Now, as citizen, no man is judge any longer of the danger to which the law requires him to expose himself, and when the prince says to him: 'It is expedient for the state that you should die', then he should die, because it is only on such terms that he has lived in security as long as he has and also because his life is no longer the bounty of nature but a gift he has received conditionally from the state.

The death-penalty inflicted on criminals may be seen in much the same way: it is in order to avoid becoming the victim of a murderer that one consents to die if one becomes a murderer oneself. Far from taking one's life under the social treaty, one thinks only of assuring it, and we shall hardly suppose that any of the contracting parties contemplates being hanged.

Moreover, since every wrongdoer attacks the society's law, he becomes by his deed a rebel and a traitor to the country; by violating its law, he ceases to be a member of it; indeed, he makes war against it. And in this case, the preservation of the state is incompatible with *his* preservation; one or the other must perish; and when the guilty man is put to death, it is less as a citizen than as an enemy. Trial and judgement are the proof and declaration that he has broken the social treaty, and is in consequence no longer a member of the state. And since he has accepted such membership, if only by his residence, he must either be banished into exile as a violator of the social pact or be put to death as a public enemy: such an enemy is not a fictitious person, but a man, and therefore the right of war makes it legitimate to kill him.

But, it will be said, the condemnation of a criminal is an individual act. Agreed; and it follows that such duties do not pertain to the sovereign; condemnation of criminals is a right the sovereign can confer but not exercise himself. All my ideas hold together, but I cannot elaborate them all at once.

In any case, frequent punishments are a sign of weakness or slackness in the government. There is no man so bad that he cannot be made good for something. No man should be put to death, even as an example, if he can be left to live without danger to society.

As for the right of pardon, or of exempting a guilty man from the penalty prescribed by law and imposed by a judge, this belongs only to that entity which is superior to both the judge and the law, namely the sovereign; but even this right is not entirely clear and it must be exercised very seldom. In a well-governed state there are few penalties, not because there are many pardons but because there are few criminals. In a decaying state the very multiplicity of crimes assures impunity. Under the Roman Republic neither the senate nor the consuls ever attempted to pardon criminals; nor did the people do so, though they sometimes revoked their own sentences. Frequent pardons signalize that crimes will soon need no pardon; and anyone can see what that must lead to. However, I can feel my heart whispering and restraining my pen; let us leave the discussion of these questions to the just man who has never erred and has therefore had no need of pardons.

CHAPTER 6

On Law

WE have given life and existence to the body politic by the social pact; now it is a matter of giving it movement and will by legislation. For the primitive act by which the body politic is formed and united does not determine what it shall do to preserve itself.

What is good and in conformity with order is such by the very nature of things and independently of human agreements. All justice comes from God, who alone is its source; and if only we knew how to receive it from that exalted fountain, we should need neither governments nor laws. There is undoubtedly a universal justice which springs from reason alone, but if that justice is to be admitted among men it must be reciprocal. Humanly speaking, the laws of natural justice, lacking any natural sanction, are unavailing among men. In fact, such laws merely benefit the wicked and injure the just, since the just respect them while others do not do so in return. So there must be covenants and positive laws to unite rights with duties and to direct justice to its object. In the state of nature, where everything is common, I owe nothing to those to whom I have promised nothing, and I recognize as belonging to others only those things that are of no use to me. But this is no longer the case in civil society, where all rights are determined by law.

Yet what, in the last analysis, is law? If we simply try to define it in terms of metaphysical ideas, we shall go on talking without reaching any understanding; and when we have said what natural law is, we shall still not know what the law of the state is.

I have already said that the general will cannot relate to any particular object. For such a particular object is either within the state or outside the state. If it is outside, then a will which is alien to it is not general with regard to it: if the object is within the state, it forms a part of the state. Then there comes into being a relationship between the whole and the part which involves two separate entities, the part being one, and the whole, less that particular part, being the other. But a whole less a particular part is no longer a whole; and so as long as this relationship exists there is no whole but only two unequal parts, from which it follows that the will of the one is no longer general with respect to the other.

But when the people as a whole makes rules for the people as a whole, it is dealing only with itself; and if any relationship emerges, it is between the entire body seen from one perspective and the same entire body seen from another, without any division whatever. Here the matter concerning which a rule is made is as general as the will which makes it. And *this* is the kind of act which I call a law.

When I say that the province of the law is always general, I mean that the law considers all subjects collectively and all actions in the abstract; it does not consider any individual man or any specific action. Thus the law may well lay down that there shall be privileges, but it may not nominate the persons who shall have those privileges; the law may establish several classes of citizen, and even specify the qualifications which shall give access to those several classes, but it may not say that this man or that shall be admitted; the law may set up a royal government and an hereditary succession, but it may not elect a king or choose a royal family – in a word, no function which deals with the individual falls within the province of the legislative power.

On this analysis, it is immediately clear that we can no longer ask *who* is to make laws, because laws are acts of the general will; no longer ask if the prince is above the law, because he is a part of the state; no longer ask if the law can be unjust, because no one is unjust to himself; and no longer ask how we can be both free and subject to laws, for the laws are but registers of what we ourselves desire.

It is also clear that since the law unites universality of will with universality of the field of legislation, anything that any man, no matter who, commands on his own authority is not a law; even what the sovereign itself commands with respect to a particular object is not a law but a decree, not an act of sovereignty but an act of government.

Any state which is ruled by law I call a 'republic', whatever the form of its constitution; for then, and then alone, does the public interest govern and then alone is the 'public thing' – the *res publica* – a reality. All legitimate government is 'republican',* I shall explain later what government is.

* By this word I understand not only an aristocracy or democracy, but generally any government directed by the general will, which is law. If it is to be legitimate, the government must not be united with the sovereign, but must serve it as its ministry. So even a monarchy can be a republic. This will be clarified in Book III.

Laws are really nothing other than the conditions on which civil society exists. A people, since it is subject to laws, ought to be the author of them. The right of laying down the rules of society belongs only to those who form the society; but how can they exercise it? Is it to be by common agreement, by a sudden inspiration? Has the body politic an organ to declare its will? Who is to give it the foresight necessary to formulate enactments and proclaim them in advance, and how is it to announce them in the hour of need? How can a blind multitude, which often does not know what it wants, because it seldom knows what is good for it, undertake by itself an enterprise as vast and difficult as a system of legislation? By themselves the people always will what is good, but by themselves they do not always discern it. The general will is always rightful, but the judgement which guides it is not always enlightened. It must be made to see things as they are, and sometimes as they should be seen; it must be shown the good path which it is seeking, and secured against seduction by the desires of individuals; it must be given a sense of situation and season, so as to weigh immediate and tangible advantages against distant and hidden evils. Individuals see the good and reject it; the public desires the good but does not see it. Both equally need guidance. Individuals must be obliged to subordinate their will to their reason; the public must be taught to recognize what it desires. Such public enlightenment would produce a union of understanding and will in the social body, bring the parts into perfect harmony and lift the whole to its fullest strength. Hence the necessity of a lawgiver.

CHAPTER 7

The Lawgiver

To discover the rules of society that are best suited to nations, there would need to exist a superior intelligence, who could understand the passions of men without feeling any of them, who had no affinity with our nature but knew it to the full, whose happiness was independent of ours, but who would nevertheless make our happiness his concern, who would be content to wait in the fullness of time for a distant glory, and to labour in one age to enjoy the fruits in another.* Gods would be needed to give men laws.

The same reasoning which Caligula used empirically, Plato used philosophically in his dialogue *The Statesman* to reach a definition of civil or kingly man. But if it is true that great princes seldom appear, how much more rare must a great lawgiver be? A prince has only to follow a model which the lawgiver provides. The lawgiver is the engineer who invents the machine; the prince is merely the mechanic who sets it up and operates it. Montesquieu says that at the birth of political societies, it is the leaders of the republic who shape the institutions but that afterwards it is the institutions which shape the leaders of the republic.

ʃ Whoever ventures on the enterprise of setting up a people must be ready, shall we say, to change human nature, to transform each individual, who by himself is entirely complete and solitary, into a part of a much greater whole, from which that same individual will then receive, in a sense, his life and his being. The founder of nations must weaken the structure

* A people does not become famous until its constitution begins to decline. We do not know for how many centuries the constitution of Lycurgus gave happiness to the Spartans before there was talk about them in the rest of Greece.

of man in order to fortify it, to replace the physical and in-dependent existence we have all received from nature with a moral and communal existence. In a word each man must be stripped of his own powers, and given powers which are external to him, and which he cannot use without the help of others.\The nearer men's natural powers are to extinction or annihilation, and the stronger and more lasting their acquired powers, the stronger and more perfect is the social institution. So much so, that if each citizen can do nothing whatever except through cooperation with others, and if the acquired power of the whole is equal to, or greater than, the sum of the natural powers of each of the individuals, then we can say that law-making has reached the highest point of perfection.

The lawgiver is, in every respect, an extraordinary man in the state. Extraordinary not only because of his genius, but equally because of his office, which is neither that of the government nor that of the sovereign. This office which gives the republic its constitution has no place in that constitution. It is a special and superior function which has nothing to do with empire over men; for just as he who has command over men must not have command over laws, neither must he who has command over laws have command over men; otherwise, the laws, in ministering to the legislator's passions, would often merely perpetuate his injustices, and partial judgements would inevitably vitiate the sanctity of his works.

When Lycurgus gave laws to his country, he began by abdicating his monarchical functions. It was the habit of most Greek cities to confer on foreigners the task of framing their laws. The modern republics of Italy have often copied this custom; the republic of Geneva did so, and found that it worked well.* Rome in its happiest age saw all the crimes of

* Those who think of Calvin merely as a theologian do not realize the extent of his genius. The codification of our wise edicts, in which he had a large share, does him as much credit as his *Institutes*. Whatever revolutions may take

the Tyranny revived within its borders, and came near to perishing simply because it had put both the legislative authority and the sovereign power in the same hands.

And yet even the decemvirs themselves never arrogated the right to make any law on their own authority alone. 'Nothing we propose to you,' they said to the people, 'can become law without your consent. Romans, be yourselves the authors of the laws which are to ensure your happiness.'

Thus the man who frames the laws ought not to have any legislative right, and the people itself cannot, even should it wish, strip itself of this untransferable right; for, according to the fundamental compact, it is only the general will which compels individuals and there can be no assurance that an individual will is in conformity with the general will until it has submitted to the free suffrage of the people – I have said this already, but it is worth repeating.

And so we find in the work of the lawgiver two things which look contradictory – a task which is beyond human powers and a non-existent authority for its execution.

There is another difficulty which deserves mention. Those sages who insist on speaking in their own language to the vulgar instead of in the vulgar language will not be understood. For there are thousands of ideas which cannot be translated into the popular idiom. Perspectives which are general and goals remote are alike beyond the range of the common herd; it is difficult for the individual, who has no taste for any scheme of government but that which serves his private interest, to appreciate the advantages to be derived from the lasting austerities which good laws impose. For a newly formed people to understand wise principles of politics and to follow the basic rules of statecraft, the effect would

___

place in our church, the memory of that great man will not cease to be honoured among the adepts of that religion while the love of country and of liberty still lives among us.

have to become the cause; the social spirit which must be the product of social institutions would have to preside over the setting up of those institutions; men would have to have already become before the advent of law that which they become as a result of law. And as the lawgiver can for these reasons employ neither force nor argument, he must have recourse to an authority of another order, one which can compel without violence and persuade without convincing.

It is this which has obliged the founders of nations throughout history to appeal to divine intervention and to attribute their own wisdom to the Gods; for then the people, feeling subject to the laws of the state as they are to those of nature, and detecting the same hand in the creation of both man and the nation, obey freely and bear with docility the yoke of the public welfare.

A sublime reason, which soars above the heads of the common people, produces those rules which the lawgiver puts into the mouth of the immortals, thus compelling by divine authority persons who cannot be moved by human prudence.* But it is not for every man to make the Gods speak, or to gain credence if he pretends to be an interpreter of the divine word. The lawgiver's great soul is the true miracle which must vindicate his mission. Any man can carve tablets of stone, or bribe an oracle, claim a secret intercourse with some divinity, train a bird to whisper in his ear, or discover some other vulgar means of imposing himself on the people. A man who can do such things may conceivably bring together a company of fools, but he will never establish an empire, and his bizarre creation will perish with him. Worthless authority may set up transitory bonds, but only wisdom

---

* 'The truth is,' writes Machiavelli, 'that there has never been in any country an extraordinary legislator who has not invoked the deity; for otherwise his laws would not have been accepted. A wise man knows many useful truths which cannot be demonstrated in such a way as to convince other people.' (*Discourses on Livy*, Book v, Chapter xi.) [In Italian in original. *Trans.*]

makes lasting ones. The Law of the Hebrews, which still lives, and that of the child of Ishmael which has ruled half the world for ten centuries, still proclaim today the greatness of the men who first enunciated them; and even though proud philosophy and the blind spirit of faction may regard them as nothing but lucky impostors, the true statesman sees, and admires in their institutions, the hand of that great and powerful genius which lies behind all lasting things.

Even so, we must not conclude from this, with Warburton, that religion and politics have the same purpose among men; it is simply that at the birth of nations, the one serves as the instrument of the other.

CHAPTER 8

The People

Just as an architect who puts up a large building first surveys and tests the ground to see if it can bear the weight, so the wise lawgiver begins not by laying down laws good in themselves, but by finding out whether the people for whom the laws are intended is able to support them. Such reasoning led Plato to refuse to provide laws for the Arcadians or the Cyreneans, because he well knew that those peoples, being rich, would not tolerate equality. Crete, too, provides an example of good laws and bad men, for the people Milos tried to discipline were dominated by their vices.

The world has seen a thousand splendid nations that could not have accepted good laws, and even those that might have accepted them could have done so only for short periods of their long history. Nations,* like men, are teachable only in their youth; with age they become incorrigible. Once customs are established and prejudices rooted, reform is a dangerous

* [Altered in Edition of 1782 to 'Most nations . . .' *Trans.*]

and fruitless enterprise; a people cannot bear to see its evils touched, even if only to be eradicated; it is like a stupid, pusillanimous invalid who trembles at the sight of a physician.

I am not denying that just as certain afflictions unhinge men's minds and banish their memory of the past, so there are certain violent epochs and revolutions in states which have the same effect on peoples that psychological shocks may have on individuals; only instead of forgetting the past, they look back on it in horror, and then the state, after being consumed by civil war, is born again, so to speak, from its own ashes, and leaps from the arms of death to regain the vigour of youth. Such was the experience of Sparta at the time of Lycurgus, of Rome after the Tarquins, and, in the modern world, of Holland and Switzerland after the expulsion of the tyrants.

But such events are unusual; they are exceptional cases to be explained by the special constitution of the states concerned. It could not even happen twice to the same people; because although a people can make itself free while it is still uncivilized, it cannot do so when its civil energies are worn out. Disturbances may well destroy a civil society without a revolution being able to restore it, so that as soon as the chains are broken, the state falls apart and exists no longer; then what is needed is a master, not a liberator. Free peoples, remember this maxim: liberty can be gained, but never *regained*.

For nations, as for men, there is a time of maturity which they must reach before they are made subject to law; but the maturity of a people is not always easily recognized; and something done too soon will prove abortive.* Peoples differ; one is amenable to discipline from the beginning; another is not, even after ten centuries. The Russians have never been

---

* [In the Edition of 1782, this sentence is revised as follows: 'Youth is not childhood. For nations, as for men, there is a time of youth or, if you prefer, of maturity which they must reach before they are made subject to law . . .' *Trans.*]

effectively governed because the attempt to govern them was made too early. Peter the Great had the talent of a copyist; he had no true genius, which is creative and makes everything from nothing. Some of the things he did were sound; most were misguided. He saw that his people was uncivilized, but he did not see that it was unready for government; he sought to civilize his subjects when he ought rather to have drilled them. He tried to turn them into Germans or Englishmen instead of making them Russians. He urged his subjects to be what they were not and so prevented them from becoming what they might have been. This is just how a French tutor trains his pupil to shine for a brief moment in his childhood and then grow up into a nonentity. The Russian Empire would like to subjugate Europe and will find itself subjugated. The Tartars, its subjects or neighbours, will become its masters – and ours. Such a revolution seems to me inevitable. All the kings of Europe are labouring in concert to hasten its coming.

CHAPTER 9

The People: Continued

JUST as nature has set bounds to the stature of a well-formed man, outside which he is either a giant or a dwarf, so, in what concerns the best constitution for a state, there are limits to the size it can have if it is to be neither too large to be well-governed nor too small to maintain itself. In the body politic there is a maximum of strength which must not be exceeded, and which is often fallen short of as a result of expansion. The more the social bond is stretched, the slacker it becomes; and in general a small state is relatively stronger for its size than a large one.

A thousand considerations bear witness to the truth of this. First, administration becomes more difficult over great distances, just as a weight becomes heavier at the end of a long lever. Government becomes more burdensome as the area is enlarged, for each town has its own administration, which the people pays for, and each region has its administration, which the people also pays for, then each province has one, and so on up to the greater governments, the satrapies, the vice-royalties, each costing more the higher they rise and always paid for by the unfortunate populace; and then on top of all comes the supreme administration, bearing down on everyone. Such a great number of charges added to charges continually exhausts the subjects; and far from being better governed by this hierarchy of orders, they are much worse off than they would be if they had only one administration over them. As it is, there is hardly any public revenue available for emergencies, and when the state is faced with such a need, it trembles on the verge of ruin.

Nor is this all. Not only is the government less vigorous and swift in enforcing respect for the law, in preventing nuisances, correcting abuses and thwarting any seditious movements that may arise in distant quarters, but at the same time the people has less feeling for governors whom it never sees, for a homeland that seems as vast as the world, and for fellow-citizens who are mostly strangers. The same laws will not suit so many various provinces, which, with their different customs and contrasting climates, cannot tolerate the same form of government. Having different laws only creates misunderstanding and confusion among peoples who live under the same governors and are in continuous communication with one another; they intermingle and intermarry, but if different sets of rules prevail, they will not even know if what they call their patrimony is really their own. Talents are hidden, virtues are ignored and vices remain unpunished when such a multitude of men, who do not know one another, is brought together in the same place by one single seat of supreme administration. The governors have too much to do to see everything for themselves; their clerks rule the state. And the measures needed to maintain a general authority, which so many scattered officials try to evade or exploit, absorb all political attention, so none is left to study the people's happiness, and hardly any left for its defence in case of need. This body which is too big for its constitution collapses and perishes, crushed by its own weight.

On the other hand, a state if it is to have strength must give itself some solid foundation, so that it can resist the shocks that it is bound to experience and sustain the exertions that it must make to preserve itself; for all peoples generate a kind of centrifugal force, by which they brush continuously against one another, and they all attempt to expand at the expense of their neighbours, like the vortices of Descartes. Thus the weak are always in danger of being swallowed up, and indeed no people can well preserve itself except by achieving a kind of equilibrium with all the others which makes the pressure everywhere the same for all.

This shows us that there are reasons for expansion and reasons for contraction; and indeed it is not the least part of political wisdom to judge, as between the one and the other, the precise balance which is most conducive to the preservation of the state. In general one might say that any reasons for expansion, which are exterior and relative, ought to be less compelling than the reasons for contraction, which are internal and absolute. A strong and healthy constitution is the first thing to look for because the strength which comes from good government is more reliable than the resources which large territories yield.

One may add that there have been states whose political structure was such that the necessity of conquest was part of their very constitution, states which, in order to maintain themselves at all, were obliged to enlarge themselves unceasingly. Possibly they have congratulated themselves on this, as a fortunate necessity; but reflection on the same necessity must also have shown them that at the end of their greatness lay the inevitable moment of their fall.

CHAPTER 10

The People: Continued

THERE are two ways of measuring a body politic, by the extent of its territory and by the number of its people; and there must be a certain balance between these two dimensions if the state is to achieve its best size. Men make the state and the soil nourishes men; thus the right balance requires that there be land enough to feed the inhabitants and as many inhabitants as the land can feed. It is in this proportion that the maximum strength of a given number of persons is brought forth; for if there is too much territory, defence is burdensome, cultivation inadequate and produce excessive; and this soon becomes the cause of defensive wars; while if, on the other hand, there is too little land, the state must live on what it can import at the discretion of its neighbours, and this soon becomes the cause of offensive wars. Any people which has to choose between commerce and war is essentially weak; it depends on its neighbours; it depends on contingencies; it will never have more than a short, uncertain existence; either it conquers and ends its predicament, or it is conquered and exists no more. It can safeguard itself in freedom only by means of littleness or bigness.

One cannot specify the exact mathematical proportion there should be between the area of the land and the number of inhabitants, because of the different characteristics of different places, differences in degrees of fertility, in the nature of the produce, in the effects of climate; and also because of the differences there are between the temperaments of men who inhabit the different territories, some consuming little in a fertile country and others living well off a frugal soil. Again we should have to consider the greater or lesser fecundity of the women, the distinctive features of the land, whether more or less favourable to population; the number of immigrants that the lawgiver might hope to attract by his institutions. From this it follows that he must make his decisions in the light not of what he sees, but of what he foresees, calculating not so much the number of the existing population as the number which the population must naturally reach. Finally, there are a thousand occasions when some particular accident of situation demands or allows the assimilation of more land than appears necessary. In a mountainous country, where the type of cultivation – woodland and pastures – requires less work, where the women are shown by experience to be more fecund than in the plains, and where the steep slopes of hills leave only a marginal degree of that flat land which alone can be relied on for vegetation, men will spread out more widely. The contrary is the case on the edge of the sea, where men will draw together in a small area, even among rocks and sands that are almost barren; for fishing can make up for much of the deficiency of agricultural produce; and being close together enables such men the better to resist pirates; and they can easily rid themselves by overseas settlement of any surplus population.

There is yet another condition for the institution of a people, one condition which no other can replace and without which all the rest are unavailing: a plenitude of peace must be enjoyed; for the period of the formation of a state, like that of the lining up of a regiment, is the time when it is least capable of resistance and most open to destruction. A state can defend itself more effectively amid total chaos than during the time of fermentation, when everyone is thinking about his own position and not about the common danger. If there is a war, famine or sedition during this critical period, the state will inevitably be overthrown.

It is true that many governments have been set up during such disturbances, but then it is the governments themselves which destroy the state. Usurpers always choose troubled times to enact, in the atmosphere of general panic, laws which the public would never adopt when passions were cool. One of the surest ways of distinguishing the work of a lawgiver from that of a tyrant is to note the moment he chooses to give a people its constitution.

Which people, then, is fit to receive laws? I answer: a people which, finding itself already bound together by some original association, interest or agreement, has not yet borne the yoke of law; a people without deep-rooted customs or superstitions; one which does not fear sudden invasion, and which, without intervening in the quarrels of its neighbours, can stand up to any of them, or secure the help of one to resist another; a people in which every member may be known to all; where there is no need to burden any man with more than he can bear; a people which can do without other peoples and which other peoples can do without;* one which is neither rich nor poor, but has enough to keep itself; and lastly one which combines the cohesion of an ancient people with the malleability of a new one. What makes the task of the lawgiver so difficult is less what has to be established than what has to be destroyed; and what makes success so rare is the impossibility of finding the simplicity of nature

* If two neighbouring peoples cannot do without one another the situation is hard for the one and dangerous for the other. Any wise nation, in such a case, will hasten to deliver the other from its dependence. The republic of Thlascala, an enclave within the Mexican Empire, preferred to do without salt rather than buy it from the Mexicans, rather even than take it from them when it was offered as a gift. The wise Thlascalians saw the trap concealed in the Mexican generosity. They kept their freedom; and their little state, locked within the territory of a great Empire, was in the end the instrument of that Empire's ruin.

together with the needs that society creates. It is difficult to combine all these conditions; and that is why so few well-constituted states exist.

There is still one country in Europe which is fit to receive laws, and that is the island of Corsica. The valour and fidelity with which this brave people has recovered and defended its freedom entitle it to be taught by some wise man how to preserve that freedom. I have a presentiment that this little island will one day astonish Europe.

CHAPTER II

Various Systems of Law

IF we enquire wherein lies precisely the greatest good of all, which ought to be the goal of every system of law, we shall find that it comes down to two main objects, *freedom* and *equality*: freedom because any individual dependence means that much strength withdrawn from the body of the state, and equality because freedom cannot survive without it.

I have already explained what civil freedom is; as for equality, this word must not be taken to imply that degrees of power and wealth should be absolutely the same for all, but rather that power shall stop short of violence and never be exercised except by virtue of authority and law, and, where wealth is concerned, that no citizen shall be rich enough to buy another and none so poor as to be forced to sell himself; this in turn implies that the more exalted persons need moderation in goods and influence and the humbler persons moderation in avarice and covetousness.*

* Do you want coherence in the state? Then bring the two extremes as close together as possible; have neither very rich men nor beggars, for these two estates, naturally inseparable, are equally fatal to the common good; from the one class come friends of tyranny, from the other, tyrants. It is always these two classes which make commerce of the public freedom: the one buys, the other sells.

Such equality, we shall be told, is a chimera of theory and could not exist in reality. But if abuse is inevitable, ought we not then at least to control it? Precisely because the force of circumstance tends always to destroy equality, the force of legislation ought always to tend to preserve it.

However, these general objectives of all institutions must be modified in each country to meet local conditions and suit the character of the people concerned. It is in the light of such factors that one must assign to each people the particular form of constitution which is best, not perhaps in itself, but for that state for which it is destined. For example, is your soil meagre and barren or the territory too narrow for its inhabitants? Then look to industry and crafts, so that manufactured goods may be exchanged for the natural resources that are lacking. Suppose, on the other hand, you have rich plains and fertile slopes, good land too little inhabited. Then concentrate on agriculture, to increase the population, and eschew artisanry, which invariably depopulates the countryside and brings the few inhabitants there are together in certain urban centres.* Have you a long and convenient coastline? Then fill the sea with ships, develop trade and navigation, and you will have a brilliant if short existence. Does the sea, along your shores, wash against almost inaccessible rocks? Then remain ichthyphagous barbarians; you will live more peacefully, better perhaps, and certainly more happily. In short, apart from those principles which are common to all, each people has its own special reasons for ordering itself in a certain way and for having laws that are fitted to itself alone. Thus it was, in the past, that the Hebrews, and more recently the Arabs, took religion as their chief object, while the Athenians had

---

* Any branch of foreign trade, says the Marquis d'Argenson, brings only an illusory advantage to the kingdom in general; it may enrich a few individuals, even a few big towns, but the nation as a whole gains nothing and the people is none the better for it.

97

literature, Carthage and Tyre trade, Rhodes seafaring, Sparta war, and Rome civic virtue. The author of *L'Esprit des lois* has shown with scores of examples how the art of the lawgiver directs the constitution towards each of its ends.

What makes the constitution of a state really strong and durable is such a close observance of conventions that natural relations and laws come to be in harmony on all points, so that the law, shall we say, seems only to ensure, accompany and correct what is natural. But if the lawgiver mistakes his object and builds on principles that differ from what is demanded by the circumstances; if his principle tends towards servitude while circumstances tend towards liberty, the one towards wealth and the other towards increased population, the one towards peace and the other towards conquest, then the laws will be weakened imperceptibly, the constitution will deteriorate, and the state will continue to be disturbed until it is finally destroyed or transformed, and invincible Nature regains her empire.

CHAPTER 12

Classification of Laws

FOR everything to be well ordered and the best possible form given to the republic, there are various relations to be considered. First, there is the action of the whole body politic on itself, that is to say, the relation of all with all, or of the sovereign with the state, and this relation, as we shall see, is made up of relations between intermediate terms.

The laws which regulate this relation bear the name of Political Laws, and are also called Fundamental Laws – not unreasonably, if the laws are wise ones. For if in each state there is only one good way of regulating it, the people which has found that way ought to keep to it. But if the established order is bad, why should the laws which prevent its being good be regarded as fundamental? Besides, a people is in any case entirely at liberty to alter its laws, even its best laws; and if it chooses to do itself an injury, who has the right to prevent it from doing so?

The second relation is that of the members of the body politic among themselves, or of each with the entire body: their relations among themselves should be as limited, and relations with the entire body as extensive, as possible, in order that each citizen shall be at the same time perfectly independent of all his fellow citizens and excessively dependent on the republic – this result is always achieved by the same means, since it is the power of the state alone which makes the freedom of its members. It is from this second relationship that Civil Laws are born.

We may consider a third kind of relation between the person and the law, namely that of disobedience and its penalty. It is this which gives rises to the establishment of Criminal Laws, though at bottom these are less a specific kind of law than the sanction behind all laws.

To these three sorts of law must be added a fourth, the most important of all, which is inscribed neither on marble nor brass, but in the hearts of the citizens, a law which forms the true constitution of the state, a law which gathers new strength every day and which, when other laws age or wither away, reanimates or replaces them; a law which sustains a nation in the spirit of its institution and imperceptibly substitutes the force of habit for the force of authority. I refer to morals, customs and, above all, belief: this feature, unknown to our political theorists, is the one on which the success of all the other laws depends; it is the feature on which the great lawgiver bestows his secret care, for though he seems to confine himself to detailed legal enactments, which are really only the arching of the vault, he knows that morals, which develop more slowly, ultimately become its immovable keystone.

Among these various classes of law, it is only Political Laws, which constitute the form of government, that are relevant to my subject.

BOOK III

Before speaking of the various forms of government, let us try to fix the precise meaning of this word, which has not hitherto been very well explained.

CHAPTER I

Of Government in General

I must warn the reader that this chapter should be read with care, for I have not the skill to make myself clear to those who do not wish to concentrate their attention.

Every free action has two causes which concur to produce it, one moral – the will which determines the act, the other physical – the strength which executes it. When I walk towards an object, it is necessary first that I should resolve to go that way and secondly that my feet should carry me. When a paralytic resolves to run and when a fit man resolves not to move, both stay where they are. The body politic has the same two motive powers – and we can make the same distinction between will and strength, the former is *legislative power* and the latter *executive power*. Nothing can be, or should be, done in the body politic without the concurrence of both.

We have seen that the legislative power belongs, and can only belong, to the people. On the other hand, it is easy to see from principles established above [Book II, Chapters 4 and 6] that executive power cannot belong to the generality of the people as legislative or sovereign, since executive power is exercised only in particular acts which are outside the province of law and therefore outside the province of the sovereign which can act only to make laws.

The public force thus needs its own agent to call it together and put it into action in accordance with the instructions of the general will, to serve also as a means of communication between the state and the sovereign, and in a sense to do for the public person what is done for the individual by the union of soul and body. This is the reason why the state needs a government, something often unhappily confused with the sovereign, but of which it is really only the minister.

What, then, is the government? An intermediary body established between the subjects and the sovereign for their mutual communication, a body charged with the execution of the laws and the maintenance of freedom, both civil and political.

The members of this body are called magistrates or *kings*, that is to say *governors*, and the whole body bears the name of *prince*.* Thus, those theorists who deny that the act by which a people submits itself to leaders is a contract are wholly correct. For that act is nothing other than a commission, a form of employment in which the governors, as simple officers of the sovereign, exercise in its name the power it has placed in their hands, a power which the sovereign can limit, modify and resume at pleasure, since the alienation of such a right would be incompatible with the nature of the social body and contrary to the purpose of the social union.

I therefore call 'government' or 'supreme administration' the legitimate exercise of the executive power, and I call 'prince' or 'magistrate' the man or the body charged with that administration.

It is in the government that we may discern those intermediary forces whose relations constitute those of all with all, or of the sovereign with the state. This last relation can be

* Thus in Venice the ruling college is called the Most Serene Prince even when the Doge is not present.

depicted as one between the extremes of a continuous proportion, of which the geometrical mean is the government. The government receives from the sovereign the orders which it gives to the people; and if the state is to be well balanced, it is necessary, all things being weighed, that the product and power of the government considered in itself should equal the product and power of the citizens who are sovereign in one sense and subjects in another.

Furthermore, no one of these three factors can be changed without destroying the balance. If the sovereign seeks to govern, or if the magistrate seeks to legislate, or if the subjects refuse to obey, then order gives way to chaos, power and will cease to act in concert, and the state, disintegrating, will lapse either into despotism or into anarchy. Lastly, as there is only one geometrical mean between two extremes, there is only one good government possible for any state; but as a thousand events may change the relations within a nation, different governments may not only be good for different peoples, but good for the same people at different times.

To try to give some idea of the various relations which may exist between the two extremes, I shall take as an example the number of the people, as this is a relation easily expressed.

Suppose the state is made up of ten thousand citizens. The sovereign can only be considered collectively and as a body, but every member as a subject has to be considered as an individual. Thus the sovereign is to the subject as ten thousand is to one, that is to say, each single member of the state has for his own share only a ten-thousandth part of the sovereign authority, although he submits himself entirely to it. Now if the people is increased to a hundred thousand men, the position of the subject is unaltered, for each bears equally with the rest the whole empire of the laws, while as sovereign his share of the suffrage is reduced to one hundred-thousandth, so that he has ten times less influence in the formulation of the laws. Hence, as the subject remains always one single individual, the ratio of sovereign to subject increases according to the number of citizens. Whence it follows that the more the state is enlarged, the more freedom is diminished.

When I say that the ratio increases, I mean that it is farther removed from parity. So the greater the ratio in the geometrical sense, the smaller the ratio in the popular sense; for in the former, the ratio, considered according to quantity, is measured by the quotient, whereas in the latter, the ratio, considered according to identity, is judged by similarity.

The smaller the ratio between the particular wills and the general will, that is, between the people's morals and the law, the more will repressive force have to be employed. Hence, for the government to be good, its strength must be increased to the extent that the people is more numerous.

In proportion as the enlargement of the state means offering the holders of public authority more temptations and more opportunities to abuse their power, it follows that the more power the government needs to control the people, the more power the sovereign needs, in its turn, to control the government. I am speaking here not of an absolute power, but of the relative power of the different elements in the state.

It follows from this double ratio that the continuous proportion between sovereign, prince and people is by no means an arbitrary idea, but a necessary consequence of the nature of the body politic. It follows further that since one of the extremes, namely the people as subject, is represented by unity, every time the double ratio is increased or diminished, the simple ratio increases or diminishes in the same way, and the middle term is in consequence changed. This shows that there is no one unique and absolute constitution of government, but that there may be as many different kinds of government as there are states of different sizes.

If anyone, wishing to ridicule this system, suggested that in order to find the geometrical mean and construct the body of the government one need only on my view take the square root of the number of the people, I should reply that I am here using that number only as an example; and the ratios of which I speak are not measured merely by the number of men but more generally by the amount of activity, which results from the concurrence of innumerable causes; I should add that although I have borrowed momentarily for the sake of expressing myself in fewer words, the language of geometry, I am still well aware that geometrical precision has no place in moral calculations.

The government is in small what the body politic (which includes it) is in large. It is a fictitious person endowed with certain faculties, active like the sovereign, passive like the state; and it can be broken down into similar relations; in consequence these relations yield a new ratio; and within each we can continue the process of analysis according to the order of the magistracies until we reach a single indivisible middle term, that is, a single chief or supreme magistrate, who may be shown at the centre of this pattern, as the unity between the series of fractions and the series of whole numbers.

Without burdening ourselves with such a multiplication of terms, let us simply consider the government as a new body within the state, distinct from both people and sovereign and intermediary between the two.

There is this essential difference between the two bodies – the state exists in itself while the government exists only through the sovereign. Thus the dominant will of the prince is, or ought to be, only the general will or the law, and his force nothing other than the public force concentrated in his hands; as soon as he resolves to perform on his own authority some absolute and independent act, the union of all begins to slacken. And if in the end it comes about that the prince has a particular will more active than that of the sovereign, and if, to enforce obedience to this particular will, he uses the public force which is in his hands, with the result that there are, so to speak, two sovereigns, one *de jure* and the other *de facto*, then the social bond vanishes at once and the body politic is dissolved.

Even so, for the body of the government to have an existence, a real life distinct from the body of the state, and for all its members to be able to act in concert and serve the purpose for which the government has been set up, it must have a particular *ego*, a consciousness common to its members, a force, a will of its own tending to its preservation. Such a particular existence implies assemblies, councils, a power to deliberate and determine rights, titles, and privileges which belongs exclusively to the prince, and which should make the position of the magistrate the more honourable in proportion to the extent to which it is the more arduous. The difficulty is to find a method of ordering this subordinate whole within the greater whole, so that it does not weaken the general constitution while strengthening its own, and so that its private force, designed for its own preservation, shall always be distinct from the public force, designed for the preservation of the state; in short, so that it will always be ready to sacrifice the government to the people and not the people to the government.

Moreover, even though the artificial body of the government is the work of another equally artificial body, and even though it has only a kind of borrowed and subordinate life, this does not prevent its being able to act with greater or less vigour and speed, and enjoying, so to speak, a health that may be more robust or less. Lastly, without departing directly from the purposes for which it has been set up, it may deviate from them in varying degrees according to the manner in which it has been constituted.

It is all these differences which give rise to the various relations that ought to exist between the government and the body of the state, in accordance with the fortuitous and particular relations by which this same state is changed. For often the government which is in itself the best becomes the most evil unless its relations with the state are modified to meet the defects of the body politic to which it belongs.

CHAPTER 2

The Constitutive Principle of the Different Forms of Government

To explain the general reason for these differences, it is necessary to distinguish here between the prince and the government, as I have already distinguished between the state and the sovereign.

The body of the magistrates may be composed of a greater or lesser number of members. We have already observed that the ratio of sovereign to subjects is greater to the extent that the people are more numerous, and by an obvious analogy we can say the same of the government in relation to the magistrates.

As the total power of the government is at all times that of the state, it never varies; and from this it follows that the more force the government exerts over its own members, the less there remains for it to use over the whole people.

Hence the more numerous the magistrates, the weaker the government. As this principle is fundamental, let us try to make it clearer.

We may distinguish in the person of the magistrate three essentially different wills. First, there is the will which belongs to the individual, and tends only to his personal advantage. Secondly, there is the collective will of the magistrates; this is concerned only with the advantage of the prince, and might be called the corporate will, since it is general *vis-à-vis* the government and particular *vis-à-vis* the state of which the government is a part. Thirdly, there is the will of the people or the sovereign will, which is general both with regard to the state considered as a whole and with regard to the government considered as part of the whole.

In a perfect system of legislation, the individual or particular will would be nonexistent, the government's own corporate will very subordinate, and the general or sovereign will therefore always dominant and always the sole regulator of all the others.

In the order of nature, on the contrary, these different wills become the more active as they are the more concentrated. Hence, the general will is always the weakest, the corporate will takes second place, and the particular will comes first of all; so much so, that within the government, each member is primarily a private self, secondly a magistrate, and thirdly a citizen. This sequence is exactly the reverse of what the social order demands.

That being so, let us suppose that the government is in the hands of a single individual. Then the particular will and the corporate will will be perfectly united, and the corporate will accordingly raised to its highest possible degree of intensity. Now, since the exercise of power depends on the degree of will, and since the absolute power of the government is invariable, it follows that the most active government is that of one man.

If, on the other hand, we combine the government and the legislative authority, make the prince the sovereign, and each citizen a magistrate – then the corporate will, being merged in the general will, will be no more active than the general will, and so leave the particular will to command the totality of power. Thus the government, having always the same absolute power, will be left with a minimum of relative strength and activity.

These relations are indisputable, and other considerations add further confirmation. It is clear, for example, that each magistrate is more active within the body of the government than is each citizen within the body of the state, and hence that the particular will has more influence over the acts of the government than it has over those of the sovereign, for every magistrate is nearly always entrusted with some distinct function of government, while no citizen, taken singly, has any distinct function of sovereignty. Besides, the more the state expands, the more its real strength is increased, though not in proportion to its expansion; but while the state remains the same size, the magistrates can be multiplied without the government gaining thereby any real strength, since its strength is that of the state, which is always the same. In this way the relative strength or activity of the government diminishes without there being any possibility of its absolute or real power increasing.

Again, there is no doubt that the dispatch of public business becomes slower in proportion as there are more persons responsible for it; attaching too much importance to prudence, large bodies attach too little to luck; they miss opportunities, and they deliberate so long that they lose the profits of deliberation.

I have just shown that the government slackens to the extent that the magistrates are multiplied, and I showed earlier that the more numerous the people, the more the repressive force must increase. From this it follows that the ratio of magistrates to government should be the inverse of the ratio of subjects to sovereign; that is to say, the more the state is enlarged, the more the government must reduce its ranks, so that the number of magistrates diminishes in proportion to the increase of the people.

I should add that I am speaking here of the relative strength of the government and not the quality of its behaviour; for, on the contrary, the more numerous the magistrates, the closer their corporate will approaches the general will, while under a single magistrate that same corporate will is, as I have said, only a particular will. Thus there is lost on the one side what could be gained on the other; and the art of the lawgiver is to know how to settle the point at which the strength and the will of the government, which always stand in inverse ratio, can be combined in the proportion most beneficial to the state.

CHAPTER 3

Classification of Governments

IN the preceding chapter we saw why the different types or forms of government are distinguished according to the number of members who compose them; it remains to be seen in the present chapter how this classification is made.

First, the sovereign may put the government in the hands of the whole people, or of the greater part of the people, so that there are more citizen-magistrates than there are ordinary private citizens. This form of government is known as *democracy*.

Alternatively, the sovereign may confine the government to the hands of a few, so that there are more ordinary citizens than there are magistrates: this form of government is called *aristocracy*.

Yet again, the sovereign may concentrate the entire government in the hands of one single magistrate, from whom all the others will derive their power. This third form of government is the most common, and is called *monarchy* or royal government.

It should be noticed that all these forms, or at any rate the first two, can be had in greater or lesser degrees; they have a fairly marked elasticity. Democracy may include all the people or it may be limited so as to include only half. Aristocracy in its turn may extend to half the people or be limited to the smallest possible number. Even royal government can to some extent be shared. Sparta had always two kings according to its constitution, and the Roman Empire is known to have had as many as eight Emperors at once without it being true to say that the Empire was divided. Thus there is always a point at which each form of government overlaps the next form; and it is clear that although government has only three names, it is actually open to as many variations of form as the state has citizens.

Moreover, since a government is able in certain respects to divide itself into separate parts, one administered in one way and the other in another way, the three forms of government may be combined to yield a multitude of mixed forms, each of which it can multiply by the three simple forms.

Throughout the ages men have debated the question 'What is government?', and yet they have failed to see that each of the possible forms is the best in some cases and the worst in others.

If in each particular state the number of supreme magistrates should be in inverse ratio to the number of citizens, it follows that, in general, democratic government suits small states, aristocratic government suits states of intermediate size and monarchy suits large states. This rule follows directly from our axiom; but how are we to calculate the multitude of particular circumstances which may offer exceptions to the rule?

CHAPTER 4

Democracy

HE who makes the law knows better than anyone how it should be executed and interpreted. So it might seem that there could be no better constitution than one which united the executive power with the legislative; in fact, this very union makes that form of government deficient in certain respects, for things which ought to be kept apart are not, and the prince and the sovereign being the same person constitute, so to speak, a government without government.

It is not good that he who makes the law should execute it or that the body of the people should turn its attention away from general perspectives and give it to particular objects. Nothing is more dangerous in public affairs than the influence of private interests, and the abuse of the law by the government is a lesser evil than that corruption of the legislator which inevitably results from the pursuit of private interests. When this happens, the state is corrupted in its very substance and no reform is possible. A people which never misused the powers of government would never misuse independence, and a people which always governed itself well would not need to be governed.

In the strict sense of the term, there has never been a true democracy, and there never will be. It is contrary to the natural order that the greater number should govern and the smaller number be governed. One can hardly imagine that all the people would sit permanently in an assembly to deal with public affairs; and one can easily see that they could not appoint commissions for that purpose without the form of administration changing.

I believe indeed that one can lay down as an axiom that

when the functions of government are divided between several commissions, those with the fewest members acquire sooner or later the greatest authority, if only because the facility of dispatching business leads naturally in that direction.

Besides, how many things that are difficult to have at the same time does the democratic form of government not presuppose? First, a very small state, where the people may be readily assembled and where each citizen may easily know all the others. Secondly, a great simplicity of manners and morals, to prevent excessive business and thorny discussions. Thirdly, a large measure of equality in social rank and fortune, without which equality in rights and authority will not last long. Finally, little or no luxury; for luxury is either the effect of riches or it makes riches necessary; it corrupts both the rich and the poor; it sells the country to effeminacy and vanity; it deprives the state of all its citizens by making some the slaves of others and all the slaves of opinion.

This is why a celebrated author has made virtue the cardinal principle of a republic; for all the conditions that I have named cannot prevail without virtue. But this same great genius, having failed to make the necessary distinctions, was often wrong and sometimes obscure, and failed to see that since the sovereign authority is everywhere the same, the same principles should have a place in every well-constituted state, though to a greater or lesser extent, assuredly, according to the form of the government.

We may add that there is no government so liable to civil war and internecine strife as is democracy or popular government, for there is none which has so powerful and constant a tendency to change to another form or which demands so much vigilance and courage to maintain it unchanged. It is under this constitution, before all others, that the citizen must be armed with strength and fidelity, and repeat from the bottom of his heart every day of his life the words a virtuous

Palatine* once spoke in the Diet of Poland: '*Malo periculosam libertatem quam quietum servitium.*'†

If there were a nation of Gods, it would govern itself democratically. A government so perfect is not suited to men.

CHAPTER 5

Aristocracy

WE have here two distinct artificial persons, namely the government and the sovereign, and therefore two general wills, one belonging to all the citizens, and the other to members of the administration only. Thus, although the government may regulate its interior discipline as it pleases, it can never speak to the people except in the name of the sovereign, that is, in the name of the people itself – something that must never be forgotten.

The first societies were governed aristocratically. The heads of families deliberated on public business among themselves; the young people yielded willingly to the authority of experience. Hence the names of *priests, elders, the senate, gerontes*. The savages of North America still retain today this method of government, and they are very well governed.

But to the extent that artificial inequality came to prevail over natural inequality, riches and power‡ came to be preferred to age, and aristocracy became elective. Lastly, the bequeathing of power together with goods by fathers to their children made families patrician and so made government hereditary; and then there appeared senators aged twenty.

There are thus three types of aristocracy, natural, elective

---

* The Palatine of Posen, father of the King of Poland and Duke of Lorraine.

† 'Better freedom with danger than peace with slavery.' [*Trans.*]

‡ It is clear that the word *Optimates*, for the ancients, did not mean the best but the strongest.

and hereditary. The first is suited only to primitive peoples; the third is the worst of all governments; the second is the best, and this is aristocracy in the true sense of the word.

Aristocracy has not only the advantage of distinguishing between the sovereign and the government, it has also the advantage of selecting its magistrates. Under popular government all the citizens are born magistrates, while this other system limits itself to a small number of magistrates, every one of whom is elected,* a method which makes honesty, sagacity, experience and all the other grounds of popular preference and esteem further guarantees of wise government.

Besides, assemblies can be more easily arranged, business can be better discussed and be dispatched with more order and diligence; the credit of the state is better upheld in the eyes of foreigners by venerable senators than it is by an unknown and despised multitude.

In a word, it is the best and most natural arrangement for the wisest to govern the multitude, if we are sure that they will govern it for its advantage and not for their own. One ought never to multiply devices uselessly, or employ twenty thousand men to do what a hundred picked men could do much better. But it must be noted that the corporate interest begins at this point to direct the national energies less strictly in accordance with the general will, and that a further inevitable tendency is for a part of the executive power to escape the domain of law.

As for the circumstances which suit this form of government, it is not necessary to have the state so small or the people so simple and upright that the execution of the law follows

* It is of the utmost importance that the law should regulate the procedure of election of magistrates, for if this is left to the will of the prince, there will be no avoiding a decline into hereditary aristocracy, as happened in the Republics of Venice and Berne. The first of these two states has long since fallen into decay, while the other preserves itself only by the extreme wisdom of its senate – a very honourable and very dangerous exception to the rule.

directly from the public will, as is the case in a good democracy. Nor must the nation be so large that the magistrates, being widely scattered, have to take upon themselves some of the powers of the sovereign, each in his own region; and so begin by making themselves independent and end by becoming masters.

But if aristocracy calls for rather fewer virtues than does popular government, it still calls for virtues of its own, such as moderation among the rich and contentment among the poor; for it seems that strict equality would be out of place; it was not observed even in Sparta.

Moreover, if this form of government involves a certain inequality of wealth, that is simply so that the administration of public affairs may be entrusted to those who can best give all their time to it, and not, as Aristotle asserted, so that the rich should always be chosen. On the contrary, it is necessary that an opposite choice should occasionally teach people that merit is a more important qualification than riches for preference.

CHAPTER 6

Monarchy

So far we have considered the prince as a collective and artificial person, unified by the force of the law and acting as trustee of executive power in the state. We have now to consider that power being held in the hands of a natural person, a real man, one having the sole right to exercise it according to the law. Such a man is known as a monarch or king.

Contrary to the other administrations, where a collective being represents an individual, in this one an individual represents a collective being; so that the moral unity which constitutes the prince is at the same time a physical unity,

116

naturally bringing together those faculties which the law brings together with such difficulty in the other forms of administration.

Thus the will of the people and the will of the prince, the public force of the state and the individual power of the government, all respond to the same mover; all the levers of the machine are in the same hands; all act towards the same end; there are no conflicting movements to counteract one another, and we cannot imagine any constitution where more action would be produced by less effort. Archimedes sitting quietly on the shore and effortlessly launching a large ship is the model of a skilful monarch governing his vast kingdom from his chamber and making everything move while he himself seems motionless.

But if there is no government more vigorous than monarchy, there is also none where the particular will has more command, and more easily dominates the other wills. Everything moves towards the same end, it is true, but that end is not the public happiness; and the very strength of the administration operates continuously to the disadvantage of the state.

Kings want to be absolute, and from afar men cry out to them that the best way of becoming absolute is to make themselves loved by their people. This is a fine precept; and even in some respects a very true one. Unfortunately, it will always be laughed at in courts. The power which rests on the love of the people is undoubtedly the greatest, but is precarious and contingent; and princes will never be satisfied with it. The best kings want to be able to be bad if they feel like it without ceasing to be masters; a political sermonizer may well tell kings that since the people's force is the king's force, a king's best interest is to have the people flourishing, numerous and formidable; but kings know very well that this is not true. Their personal interest is primarily that the people should be weak, wretched and never able to resist them. I admit that if the subjects were always perfectly submissive, then it would be to the interest of the prince for the people to be strong, so that the people's strength, being also the prince's strength, should make him feared by his neighbours; but since this is only a secondary and subordinate advantage, and since strength is incompatible with submissiveness, it is natural that princes always prefer the doctrine that is more immediately useful to them. This is what Samuel put forcefully to the Hebrews, and what Machiavelli has proved very clearly – under the pretence of instructing kings, he has taught important lessons to the people. Machiavelli's *Prince* is a handbook for republicans.*

We have seen from the discussion of general proportions that monarchy is suited only to large states, and we find this again when we examine monarchy in itself. The more numerous the public administrators, the more the ratio between prince and subjects diminishes and approaches parity, coming to a point where the ratio is one to one, or equality itself, in democracy. This same ratio is greater to the extent that the government contracts, and reaches its maximum when the government is in the hands of a single man. Then there is too great a distance between the prince and the people and the state lacks bonds of union. For such bonds to be formed there must be intermediary ranks, with princelings, grandees, and a nobility to fill them. But all this is unsuited to a small state, which would be ruined by so many social orders.

---

* Machiavelli was a gentleman and a good citizen; but being attached to the house of Medici, he was forced during the oppression of his country to disguise his love of liberty. The very choice of an execrable hero reveals his secret intention, and the antithesis between his principles in his book *The Prince* and those in his *Discourses on Livy* and *The History of Florence* proves that this profound political thinker has so far had only superficial or corrupted readers. The Pope's court strictly prohibited his book, which I can well believe, since that was the Court he depicts most plainly. [Note added to the Edition of 1782.]

But if it is difficult for a large state to be well governed, it is still more difficult for it to be well governed by a single man; and everyone knows what happens when a king rules through deputies.

An essential and inevitable defect, which will always make monarchical government inferior to republican government, is that whereas in republics the popular choice almost always elevates to the highest places only intelligent and capable men, who fill their office with honour, those who rise under monarchies are nearly always muddled little minds, petty knaves and intriguers with small talents which enable them to rise to high places in courts, but which betray their ineptitude to the public as soon as they are appointed. The people is much less often mistaken in such choices than is a prince, and a man of real merit is almost as rare in a royal ministry as a fool at the head of a republican government. Thus, when by some happy chance a born ruler takes the helm of affairs in a monarchy that is almost wrecked by swarms of egregious administrators, then everyone is amazed at the resources he discovers, and his reign marks an epoch in the history of the country.

For a monarchy to be well governed, its size and extent ought to be proportionate to the talents of those who govern. It is easier to conquer than to administer. With enough leverage, a finger could overturn the world; but to support the world, one must have the shoulders of Hercules. However small the state may be, princes are almost always inadequate. When, on the other hand, it happens that the state is too small for its ruler, a very rare thing, then it is even worse governed, because such a ruler, in following his own broad vision, forgets the people's interest; and he makes them no less miserable by the misuse of his superabundant abilities than a mediocre ruler would make them through the defects of an insufficient talent. It is as if kingdoms ought, so to speak, to expand or contract with each successive reign, according to the capacity of the prince. In a republic, on the other hand, where the talents of the senate are of a more settled measure, the state can have fixed boundaries without the administration working any less well.

The most perceptible disadvantage of government by one man is the lack of that continuity of succession which provides an uninterrupted bond of union in the other two systems. When a king dies, another is needed; elections leave a dangerous interval; they are stormy; and unless the citizens have more disinterestedness and integrity than is usual under such governments, there will be bribery and corruption. It is difficult for one to whom the state has been sold not to sell it in his turn, and recover from the weak the gold which the strong have extorted from him. Sooner or later, under such an administration everything becomes venal; and the peace which is enjoyed under kings is worse than the disturbances of interregnums.

What has been done to prevent this evil? Thrones have been made hereditary in certain families, and an order of succession thus set up to prevent any dispute on the death of the king – that is to say, by substituting for the disadvantages of elections, the disadvantages of regencies, apparent peace has been preferred to wise administration, and the risk of having children or monsters or imbeciles for rulers preferred to having to dispute the choice of a good king. People do not realize that in exposing themselves to the hazards of these alternatives, they are gambling against all the odds. It was a very shrewd remark that the young Dionysus made to his father, when his father, reproaching him for a dishonourable action, said: 'Did I set you such an example?' 'Ah,' replied the son, 'your father was not a king.'

When someone is brought up to command others, everything conspires to rob him of justice and reason. Great pains are taken, we are told, to teach young princes the art of ruling;

but it does not appear that this education does them any good. It would be better to begin by teaching them the art of obeying. The greatest kings known to history were not among those brought up to rule, for ruling is a science that is least well mastered by too much practice; it is one a man learns better in obeying than in commanding. *Nam utilissimus idem ac brevissimus bonarum malarumque rerum delectus, cogitare quid aut nolueris sub alio Principe aut volueris.**

One consequence of this lack of coherence is the instability of royal government, which, being sometimes directed according to one plan and sometimes according to another, depending on the personality of the king who rules, or of those who rule for him, cannot long have a fixed objective or a consistent policy; this unsettledness makes the state drift from principle to principle, and from project to project, a defect not found in those forms of government where the prince is always the same. Thus we see that, in general, if there is more cunning in a royal court, there is more wisdom in a republican senate, and that republics have a more stable and effective guidance – something which cannot obtain where every revolution in the administration means a revolution in the state – for it is the universal rule of all ministers and nearly all kings to reverse the policy of their predecessors.

This same lack of cohesion gives the lie to a sophism which is very common among royalist political thinkers, that is, not only of comparing civil government to household government and the prince to the father of a family – a fallacy I have already refuted – but also of generously attributing to a royal ruler all the virtues he has need of, and always assuming that the prince is everything he should be. With the help of these assumptions, royal government becomes manifestly preferable

* 'The best as well as the shortest way to find out what is good and what is bad is to consider what you would have wished to happen if someone other than yourself had been Prince.' (Tacitus, *History*, Book I.) [*Trans.*]

to all other kinds, because it is incontestably the strongest, and needs only a corporate will more in harmony with the general will to be also the best form of government.

But if, according to Plato, a born king is a very rare being – how often do Nature and Fortune combine to enthrone such a man? And if a royal education necessarily corrupts those who receive it, what must be expected of a succession of men brought up to rule?

It is deliberate self-deception to confuse royal government with the government of a good king. To understand what this form of government is inherently, one must consider it as it is under mediocre or evil princes, for either princes will be such when they accede to the throne or such is what occupying the throne will make them.

Although these difficulties do not escape our authors, they have never been in the least embarrassed by them. The remedy, they say, is to obey without a murmur. God in his wrath inflicts bad kings on us, so they must be endured as a divine punishment. This argument is undoubtedly edifying; but I fancy it is more suited to the pulpit than to a book of political theory. What would be said about a physician who promised miracles, and whose whole art was to teach the sick to practise patience?

We all know that we have to put up with a bad government when it is bad; the problem is to find a good government.

CHAPTER 7

Mixed Forms of Government

STRICTLY speaking, no government of a simple form exists. A single head of state has to have subordinate magistrates; a people's government must have a head. Thus in the division of executive power there is always a gradation from the larger number to the smaller – with this difference, that sometimes the many depend on the few, and sometimes the few depend on the many.

Sometimes there is an equal division, either when the constitutive parts are mutually dependent, as in the government of England, or when the authority of each part is independent but imperfect, as in the case of Poland. This latter form is bad, because there is no unity in the government, and the state lacks bonds of union. Which is better: a simple form of government or a mixed one? This is a question much debated by political theorists, and one to which I myself must give the answer I gave earlier about all forms of government.

In itself, the simple form of government is the best, precisely because it is simple. But when the executive power is not sufficiently subordinate to the legislative – that is to say, when the ratio of prince to sovereign is greater than that of people to prince – this lack of proportion has to be remedied by dividing the government, for then all the diverse elements of the government will have no less authority over the subjects, but their separation will make them less powerful against the sovereign.

The same disadvantage can also be prevented by establishing intermediate magistrates who, separated from the government altogether, serve only to balance the two powers, and uphold their respective rights. Then the government is not mixed, it is tempered.

The opposite disadvantage can be remedied by similar means; and when the government is too slack, commissions can be set up to give it concentration. In the first case, the government is divided in order to weaken it; in the second, in order to strengthen it. This is the practice of all democracies. The maximum of strength and of weakness are equally found in the simple forms of government, whereas the mixed forms provide a moderate degree of strength.

CHAPTER 8

That All Forms of Government Do Not Suit All Countries

FREEDOM is not a fruit of every climate, and it is not therefore within the capacity of every people. The more one reflects on this doctrine of Montesquieu, the more one is conscious of its truth. And the more often it is challenged, the more opportunities are given to establish it with new evidence.

In every government in the world, the public person consumes but does not produce anything. Whence does it obtain the substance it consumes? From the labour of its members. It is the surplus of private production which furnishes public subsistence. From this it follows that the civil state can subsist only if men's work yields more than they themselves need.

But this surplus is not the same in every country of the world. In some it is substantial, in others middling, in some nil, in others a deficit. The proportion depends on the fertility of the climate, on the kind of labour which the soil requires, on the nature of its products, on the strength of the inhabitants, and on the degree of consumption that is necessary for them, and on various other factors which go to make up the whole proportion.

In addition, all governments do not have the same nature; some are more voracious than others; and their differences are based on this next principle — that the further public contributions are from their source, the more burdensome they are. This burden should not be measured by the quantity of the contributions exacted, but by the distance they have to go to return to the hands from which they come; when this circulation is rapid and well established, it does not matter whether much or little is paid; the people will always be rich and finances will flourish. Correspondingly, however little the people gives, when that little does not return to it, it soon exhausts itself in continuous payments; the state is never rich and the people is always penurious.

This demonstrates that the greater the distance between the people and the government, the more onerous the taxes become; so that in a democracy the people is least burdened, in an aristocracy more burdened, and in a monarchy it bears the greatest weight of all. Monarchy is thus suited only to opulent nations, aristocracy to those of moderate wealth and size, and democracy to small and poor countries.

Indeed, the more one reflects, the more one recognizes that in this matter there are differences between free states and monarchies: in the former everything is used for the common advantage, while in the latter, private power and public power are competitive, and the one is increased only by weakening the other. As for despotism, instead of governing the subjects in order to make them happy, it makes them miserable in order to govern them.

Thus in every climate there are natural factors on the basis of which one can determine the form of government which that climate necessitates; and we can even say what sort of inhabitants each must have.

Mean and sterile places, where the product does not repay the labour, must remain uncultivated and deserted, or peopled only by savages. Places which yield only the bare necessities of men's lives must be inhabited by barbarous peoples, since no political society is possible. Places where the surplus of product over labour is moderate are suited to free peoples. Places where an abundant and fertile soil gives a lavish return for little labour will want monarchical government, so that the luxury of the prince may consume the surplus of the product of the subjects – for it is better that this surplus should be absorbed by the government than dissipated by private persons. There are exceptions, I know, but these exceptions themselves confirm the rule, in that sooner or later they produce revolutions which put things back into the order of nature.

We must always distinguish general laws from particular causes which can modify their effect. If all the South were covered with republics and all the North with despotic states, it would still be true that, in terms of climate, despotism suits hot countries, barbarism cold countries, and that a good polity suits temperate regions. I realize that this general rule may be admitted and its application disputed; it could be argued that there are very fertile cold countries and very barren southern ones. But this is a difficulty only for those who fail to see the thing in all its ramifications. One must, as I have already said, consider the factors of production, strength, consumption and so on.

Suppose there are two equal territories, one yielding five units, the other ten. If the inhabitants of the former consume four and those of the latter nine, the surplus of the one will be one-fifth and of the other one-tenth. The ratio of these two surpluses will then be the inverse of that of their products, so that the territory yielding five units will show a surplus double that of the territory yielding ten.

But there is no question of a double product, and I do not believe anyone could venture to equate the fertility of a cold country with that of a hot country. But let us assume such equality; let us, for example, equate England and Sicily, Poland and Egypt. Farther south there will be Africa and India; farther north, there will be nothing. What differences in agricultural technique will be needed to achieve this equality of product? In Sicily, it is enough simply to scratch the soil, while in England, how much effort is needed to work it! But where more hands are required to obtain the same product, the surplus is necessarily less.

Note a further point, that the same number of men consume much less in hot countries. The climate requires a man to be abstemious to keep fit – and Europeans who try to live in hot countries as they live at home die of dysentry and stomach disorders. 'We,' says Chardin, 'are carnivorous beasts, wolves, compared to the Asians. Some attribute the abstemiousness of the Persians to the fact that their country is less cultivated; but I, on the contrary, believe that their country is less rich in commodities because the inhabitants need less. If their frugality [he continues] were the effect of the poverty of the soil, it would be the poor alone who ate little; in fact everybody does; and instead of finding people eating less or more in each province according to the fertility of the land, one finds the same frugality throughout the kingdom. They are very proud of their way of life, and say that one has only to look at their complexions to see how superior their way is to that of other nations. And indeed, the complexion of the Persians is clear, their skin is fair, delicate and smooth, while that of the Armenians, their subjects who live in the European manner, is rough and blotchy, and their bodies are fat and heavy.'

The closer men are to the equator, the more frugally they live. They eat hardly any meat; rice, maize, couscous, millet and cassava are their daily food. In India there are millions of men whose food costs less than a penny a day. In Europe itself we notice a marked difference of appetite between the peoples of the north and those of the south. A Spaniard could live eight days on the dinner of a German. In countries where men are more gluttonous, luxury is turned towards the things men consume. In England, it shows itself in tables loaded with meats; in Italy one is regaled on sugar and flowers.

Luxury in clothing reveals similar differences. In countries where the changes of season are swift and violent, people have better and simpler clothes; in countries where they dress only for appearance, people care more for show than utility, and clothes themselves are a luxury. In Naples you will see men strolling daily along the Posillipo in gold-embroidered jackets and no hose. It is the same thing with buildings; people attach importance to magnificence when they have nothing to fear from the climate. In Paris or London people want to be housed warmly and comfortably. In Madrid, they have superb reception rooms, but no windows that close and their bedrooms are like rat holes.

Foodstuffs are more substantial and richer in hot countries – this is a third difference and it does not fail to influence the second. Why does one eat so many vegetables in Italy? Because they are good, nourishing and of excellent flavour. In France, where they get nothing but water, they are not at all nourishing, and count for nothing at the table; but even so they take up no less ground and cost just as much to cultivate. Experiment has shown that the wheats of Barbary, otherwise inferior to those of France, yield much more flour; and that the French wheats, in turn, yield more than those of the North. From this one can deduce that a similar gradation may be observed along a line from the equator to the pole. Now is it not a tangible disadvantage to have a smaller amount of nourishment in an equal quantity of produce?

To all these various considerations, I may add another which is drawn from, and which reinforces them, that is, that hot countries need fewer inhabitants than cold countries, and can feed more – which provides a double surplus to the advantage of despotism. The wider the area that is occupied by the same number of people, the more difficult revolts become; for the inhabitants cannot get together quickly and secretly, while it is always easy for the government to discover plots and to cut communications. On the other hand, the more a numerous people is packed together, the less easily can the government infringe on the sovereign; popular leaders deliberate as securely in their private rooms as the prince in his council, and the crowd gathers as swiftly in the public squares as the troops in their barracks. It is thus to the advantage of tyrannical government to act over great distances. With the aid of strongpoints to serve as fulcra, its strength increases with distance, on the principle of leverage.*

The strength of the people, on the contrary, is effective only if it is concentrated; it evaporates and is lost when it is dispersed, just as gunpowder scattered on the ground ignites only grain by grain. The least populous countries are thus the most fitted to tyranny; wild beasts reign only in deserts.

CHAPTER 9

The Signs of a Good Government

WHEN, therefore, one asks what in absolute terms is the best government, one is asking a question which is unanswerable because it is indeterminate; or alternatively one might say that there are as many good answers as there are possible combinations in the absolute and relative positions of peoples.

But if it is asked by what signs one can tell whether a given people is well or badly governed, that is another matter; and the question of fact can be answered.

Even so, it is not really answered, because everyone will want to answer it in his own way. Subjects prize public tranquillity; citizens the freedom of the individual – the former prefer security of possessions, the latter security of person; subjects think the best government is the most severe, citizens

* This does not contradict what I said in Book II, Chapter 9, about the disadvantages of a large state, for there I was dealing with the authority of the government over its members, and here it is a question of the government's strength over the subjects. Its scattered members serve it as so many fulcra to exert pressure on the people from a distance, but it has no such fulcrum to exert pressure on its own members. Thus in the one case the length of the lever is its weakness; in the other, its strength.

that it is the mildest; the former want crimes to be punished, the latter want them prevented; subjects think it is a good thing to be feared by their neighbours, citizens prefer to be ignored by them; the former are satisfied so long as money circulates, the latter demand that the people shall have bread. But even if there were agreement on these and suchlike points, should we be any more advanced? Moral dimensions have no precise standard of measurement; even if we could agree about signs, how should we agree in appraisal?

For myself, I am always astonished that people should fail to recognize so simple a sign, or be so insincere as not to agree about it. What is the object of any political association? It is the protection and the prosperity of its members. And what is the surest evidence that they are so protected and prosperous? The numbers of their population. Then do not look beyond this much debated evidence. All other things being equal, the government under which, without external aids like naturalization and immigration, the citizens increase and multiply most, is infallibly the best government. That under which the people diminishes and wastes away is the worst. Statisticians, this is your problem: count, measure, compare.*

---

* One must judge on the same principle the centuries that merit preference in respect of the prosperity of the human race. People have too much admired those that have witnessed a flourishing of crafts and letters without penetrating the secret purpose of their culture, and without considering its fatal consequences, *idque apud imperitos humanitas vocabatur, cum pars servitutis esset*. Shall we never see behind the precepts of books the crude self-interest which prompts the authors to speak? No, whatever they may say, when, notwithstanding its brilliance, a country is depopulated, it is simply not true that all is going well; and it is not enough for a poet to have an income of 100,000 livres for his century to be the best of all. It is less important to consider the apparent repose and tranquillity of rulers than the wellbeing of whole nations and above all of the most populous states. A hailstorm may devastate a few cantons, but it rarely causes famine. Riots and civil wars may greatly alarm rulers, but they are not the true misfortunes of peoples, who can at least have a few months' respite during the quarrels as to who is to be the next tyrant. Their calamities and their happiness both arise from their permanent condition. When all

CHAPTER 10

The Abuse of Government and its Tendency to Degenerate

JUST as the particular will acts unceasingly against the general will, so does the government continually exert itself against the sovereign. And the more this exertion increases, the more the constitution becomes corrupt, and, as in this case there is no distinct corporate will to resist the will of the prince and so to balance it, sooner or later it is inevitable that the prince will oppress the sovereign and break the social treaty. This is the inherent and inescapable defect which, from the birth of the political body, tends relentlessly to destroy it, just as old age and death destroy the body of a man.

There are two common ways by which a government degenerates – when it itself contracts and when the state dissolves.

The government contracts when its members pass from a greater to a smaller number, that is, from democracy to aristocracy, or from aristocracy to royal government. This is

---

remain supine under the yoke, it is then that everything decays, it is then that the rulers can destroy them at their ease, *ubi solitudinem faciunt pacem appellant.* When the quarrels of the state disturbed the kingdom of France, and the Co-adjutor of Paris attended the *Parlement* with a dagger in his pocket, this did not prevent the French people living happily and multiplying in a free and decent ease. In ancient times, Greece flourished at the height of the cruellest wars; blood flowed in torrents, but the whole country was thickly populated. 'It appeared,' says Machiavelli, 'that in the midst of murder, proscription and civil wars, our republic became stronger than ever; the civil virtue of the citizens, their morals, and their independence, served more effectively to strengthen it than all their dissensions may have done to weaken it.' A little disturbance gives vigour to the soul, and what really makes the species prosper is not peace but freedom.

its natural tendency.* If it were to move in the other direction from a smaller number to a greater, the government might be said to slacken; but such an inverse progression is impossible.

For indeed, a government never changes its form unless its exhausted energies are too feeble to maintain its original form.

* The slow formation and progress of the Republic of Venice in its lagoons provides a notable example of this progression; and it is really astonishing that after more than twelve hundred years, the Venetians seem still to be at the second stage, which began with the Serrar di Consiglio in 1198. As for the ancient Doges, for whom the Venetians are reproached, whatever may be said by the *squittinio della libertà veneta*, there is proof that the Doges were not their sovereigns.

People will not fail to quote against me the case of the Roman Republic, which is said to have followed a reverse sequence, from monarchy to aristocracy and from aristocracy to democracy. But I am very far from sharing this opinion.

The first constitution of Romulus was a mixed government, which promptly degenerated into a despotism. For special reasons, the state perished before its time, just as one sometimes sees an infant die before reaching the age of maturity. The expulsion of the Tarquins was the real moment of the birth of the Republic. But it did not at first assume a fixed form, because the failure to abolish the patriciate left the task half-finished. For the hereditary aristocracy, which is the worst of all legitimate administrations, remained in conflict with democracy, and the form of government, continuously uncertain and wavering, was not fixed (as Machiavelli has proved) until the establishment of the tribunes; only then was there a true government and a true democracy. For indeed the people then was not only sovereign, but also magistrate and judge; and the senate was no more than a subordinate commission to temper and concentrate the government, while the consuls themselves – in spite of their being patricians, chief magistrates and absolute commanders in war – were never more in Rome than presidents of the people.

From that time, the government was seen to follow its natural inclination, and tend strongly towards aristocracy. The patriciate having as it were abolished itself, the aristocracy was no longer seated in the body of the patricians, as in Venice and Genoa, but in the body of the senate composed of patricians and plebeians, even in the body of the tribunes, when they began to usurp the active power. For words do not alter things, and when the people have chiefs who govern on their behalf, this is still an aristocracy no matter what name those persons bear.

The abuse of aristocracy gave birth to civil war and the triumvirate. Sulla, Julius Caesar and Augustus became in fact as good as monarchs, and finally under the despotism of Tiberius the state was dissolved. Roman history, then, does not belie my principle: it confirms it.

If it slackened while expanding, its strength would be absolutely null, and it would be even less likely to survive. It must therefore wind up and tighten the mechanism as it begins to slacken, for otherwise the state which depends on it will fall into ruin.

The dissolution of the state may take place in two ways.

First it takes place when the prince ceases to administer the state according to the law and usurps the sovereign power. Then a remarkable change occurs; for it is not the government but the state which contracts – by which I mean that the state as a whole is dissolved and another is formed inside it, one composed only of members of the government and having no significance for the rest of the people except that of a master and a tyrant. Now, at the moment the government usurps sovereignty, the social pact is broken, and all the ordinary citizens, recovering by right their natural freedom, are compelled by force, but not morally obliged, to obey.

The same situation occurs when the members of the government separately usurp the power which they ought only to exercise as a body; for this is no less an infraction of the law, and it produces an even greater disorder. For then there are, so to speak, as many princes as there are magistrates, and the state being no less divided than the government, perishes or changes its form.

When the state is dissolved, the abuse of government, whatever it may be, takes the general name of *anarchy*. More precisely democracy degenerates into *ochlocracy*, aristocracy into *oligarchy*, and I would add that royal government degenerates into *tyranny*, except that this last word is ambiguous and requires explanation.

In the commonly understood sense, a tyrant is a king who governs violently and without regard to justice and the law. In the exact sense, a tyrant is an individual who arrogates to himself royal authority without having any right to it. It is thus that the Greeks understood the word 'tyrant'. They applied it indiscriminately to good and bad princes whenever their authority was not legitimate.* Thus *tyrant* and *usurper* are perfectly synonymous words. To give different names to different things, I call a usurper of royal authority a 'tyrant' and the usurper of the sovereign power a 'despot'. The tyrant is one who intrudes, contrary to law, to govern according to the law; the despot is one who puts himself above the law. Thus the tyrant need not be a despot, but a despot is always a tyrant.

CHAPTER II

The Death of the Body Politic

SUCH is the natural and inevitable inclination of the best constituted governments. If Sparta and Rome perished, what state can hope to last for ever? If we wish, then, to set up a lasting constitution, let us not dream of making it eternal. We can succeed only if we avoid attempting the impossible and flattering ourselves that we can give to the work of man a durability that does not belong to human things.

The body politic, no less than the body of a man, begins to die as soon as it is born, and bears within itself the causes of its own destruction. Either kind of body may have a constitution of greater or less robustness, fitted to preserve it for a longer or

---

*'*Omnes enim et habentur et dicuntur Tyranni qui potestate utuntur perpetua, in ea Civitate quae libertate usa est.*' ('For all are thought and called tyrants who exercise perpetual power in a city accustomed to freedom.' Cornelius Nepos, *Life of Miltiades*.) It is true that Aristotle (*Nicomachean Ethics*, VIII, 10) distinguishes between a tyrant and a king, saying the former governs for his own advantage while the latter governs only for the advantage of his subjects; but in addition to the fact that in general all the Greek authors used the word 'tyrant' in another sense, as we see above all in the *Hiero* of Xenophon, it would follow from Aristotle's criterion, that there had never yet been a single king since the beginning of the world.

shorter time. The constitution of a man is the work of nature; that of the state is the work of artifice. It is not within the capacity of men to prolong their own lives, but it is within the capacity of men to prolong the life of the state as far as possible by giving it the best constitution it can have. And although even the best constitution will come to an end, it will do so later than any other, unless some unforeseen hazard fells it before its time.

The principle of political life dwells in the sovereign authority. The legislative power is the heart of the state, the executive power is the brain, which sets all the parts in motion. The brain may become paralysed and the individual still live. A man can be an imbecile and survive, but as soon as his heart stops functioning, the creature is dead.

It is not only through the law that the state keeps alive; it is through the legislative power. Yesterday's law is not binding today, but for the fact that silence gives a presumption of tacit consent and the sovereign is taken to confirm perpetually the laws it does not abrogate while it has power to abrogate them. Everything which it has once declared to be its will, it wills always – at least until it issues a revocation.

Why then do ancient laws command so much respect? Precisely because they are ancient. We must believe that it is only the excellence of such laws that has enabled them to last so long; if the sovereign had not continually recognized them as salutary, they would have been revoked a thousand times. This is why the laws, far from growing weaker, constantly gain new strength in every well-constituted state; the prejudice in favour of antiquity makes them every day more venerable; in those cases, on the other hand, where the laws become weaker with age, this shows that there is no longer any legislative power and that the state is dead.

CHAPTER 12

How the Sovereign Authority Maintains Itself

THE sovereign, having no other force than the legislative power, acts only through the laws, and since the laws are nothing other than authentic acts of the general will, the sovereign can act only when the people is assembled. The people assembled, it will be said – what an illusion! It is indeed an illusion today; but two thousand years ago it was not. Has human nature so much changed?

The boundaries of the possible in the moral realm are less narrow than we think; it is our own weaknesses, our vices and our prejudices that limit them. Base minds do not believe in great men; low slaves smile in mockery at the word 'freedom'.

In the light of what has been done, let us consider what can be done. I shall not speak of the ancient republics of Greece; but the Roman Republic was, it seems to me, a large state and the town of Rome a large town: the last census gave four hundred thousand men in Rome carrying arms, and the last census calculation under the Empire more than four million citizens without counting subjects, foreigners, women, children or slaves.

One would suppose that it must have been difficult to bring together frequently the numerous people of the capital and its surroundings. In fact, very few weeks passed without the Roman people being assembled, even several times in one week. This people not only exercised the rights of sovereignty, but also a part of the government. It dealt with certain business; it tried certain cases; and the entire people in the public assemblies enacted the role of magistrate almost as often as that of citizen.

Looking back to the earliest history of nations, we notice

that the majority of ancient governments, even monarchical ones like those of the Macedonians and the Franks, had similar assemblies. In any case, the one indisputable fact I have cited answers our question; it seems to me good logic to reason from the actual to the possible.

CHAPTER 13

The Same – Continued

IT is not enough that the assembled people should have once determined the constitution of the state by giving sanction to a body of laws; it is not enough that it should set up a perpetual government, or that it should have provided once and for all for the election of magistrates. In addition to the extraordinary assemblies that unforeseen events may necessitate, there must be fixed and periodic assemblies which nothing can abolish or prorogue, so that on the appointed day the people is rightfully summoned by the law itself without any further formal convocation being needed.

But apart from these assemblies which are lawful by their date alone, any assembly of the people which has not been summoned by the magistrate appointed for that duty and according to the prescribed form must be held to be unlawful, and everything it does must be void, for the order to assemble should itself emanate from the law.

As to whether legitimate assemblies should be more or less frequent, this depends on so many circumstances that one cannot lay down in advance any precise rules. One can only say that in general the more strength the government has, the more frequently the sovereign should reveal itself.

This, I shall be told, may be good for one single town, but what is to be done if the state consists of several towns? Is the sovereign authority to be divided? Or should it be concentrated in one single town holding the others as subject? I answer that neither the one thing nor the other should be done. In the first place, the sovereign authority is simple and single; it cannot be divided without being destroyed. In the second place, a town cannot legitimately be subject to another any more than a nation may be, because the essence of the political body lies in the union of freedom and obedience so that the words 'subject' and 'sovereign' are identical correlatives, the meaning of which is brought together in the single word 'citizen'.

I should answer further that it is always an evil to unite several towns in one nation, and whoever wishes to form such a union should not flatter himself that the natural disadvantages can be avoided. It is no use complaining about the evils of a large state to someone who wants only small ones. But how are small states to be given enough strength to resist large states, as the Greek cities once resisted a great king and as, more recently, Holland and Switzerland resisted the House of Austria?

Nevertheless, if the state cannot be limited to reasonable boundaries, there remains one remedy, and that is to have no fixed capital, but to move the seat of government from one place to another and to assemble the estates of the country in each in turn.

People the territory evenly, extend the same rights to everyone, carry the same abundance and life into every quarter – it is by these means that the state will become at once the strongest and the best governed that is possible. Remember that the walls of towns are made only from the debris of rural houses. Every time I see a mansion being built in the capital I fancy I can see the whole countryside covered with hovels.

CHAPTER 14

The Same – Continued

THE moment the people is lawfully assembled as a sovereign body all jurisdiction of the government ceases; the executive power is suspended, and the person of the humblest citizen is as sacred and inviolable as that of the highest magistrate, for in the presence of the represented there is no longer any representation. Most of the disturbances which took place in the Roman assemblies were the result of this rule being either unknown or neglected. The consuls were no more than the presidents of the people; the tribunes were mere speakers;* the senate was nothing at all.

These intervals of suspension, when the prince recognizes – or ought to recognize – a real superior, are always alarming for princes; and the assemblies of the people, which are the shield of the body politic and the brake on the government, have always been the nightmare of magistrates; hence the latter spare no effort in raising objections, problems, promises to turn the citizens against assemblies. When the citizens are avaricious, cowardly, pusillanimous, and love repose more than freedom, they do not hold out against the redoubled efforts of the government. It is then that, as the opposing force increases continuously, the sovereign authority atrophies in the end and the majority of republics fall and perish before their time.

But between the sovereign authority and arbitrary government there sometimes appears an intermediate power of which we must now speak.

* The word is used here somewhat in the sense it has in the English parliament. The resemblance between these functions would have caused conflict between the Consuls and the Tribunes, even if all jurisdiction had been suspended.

CHAPTER 15

Deputies or Representatives

As soon as public service ceases to be the main concern of the citizens and they come to prefer to serve the state with their purse rather than their person, the state is already close to ruin. Are troops needed to march to war? They pay mercenaries and stay at home. Is it time to go to an assembly? They pay deputies and stay at home. Thanks to laziness and money, they end up with soldiers to enslave the country and deputies to sell it.

It is the bustle of commerce and the crafts, it is the avid thirst for profit, it is effeminacy and the love of comfort that commute personal service for money. Men give up a part of their profits so as to increase the rest at their ease. Use money thus, and you will soon have chains. The word 'finance' is the word of a slave; it is unknown in the true republic. In a genuinely free state, the citizens do everything with their own hands and nothing by means of money; far from paying for exemption from their duties, they would pay to discharge them in person. I am very far from sharing received ideas: I believe that compulsory service is less contrary to liberty than is taxation.

The better the state is constituted, the more does public business take precedence over private in the minds of the citizens. There is indeed much less private business, because the sum of the public happiness furnishes a larger proportion of each individual's happiness, so there remains less for him to seek on his own. In a well-regulated nation, every man hastens to the assemblies; under a bad government, no one wants to take a step to go to them, because no one feels the least interest in what is done there, since it is predictable that the general will will not be dominant, and, in short, because domestic concerns absorb all the individual's attention. Good laws lead men to make better ones; bad laws lead to worse. As soon as someone says of the business of the state – 'What does it matter to me?' – then the state must be reckoned lost.

The cooling-off of patriotism, the activity of private interest, the vastness of states, conquests, the abuse of government – all these have suggested the expedient of having deputies or representatives of the people in the assemblies of the nation. This is what in certain countries they dare to call the third estate – the private interest of two classes being there given first and second place, and the public interest only third place.

Sovereignty cannot be represented, for the same reason that it cannot be alienated; its essence is the general will, and will cannot be represented – either it is the general will or it is something else; there is no intermediate possibility. Thus the people's deputies are not, and could not be, its representatives; they are merely its agents; and they cannot decide anything finally. Any law which the people has not ratified in person is void; it is not law at all. The English people believes itself to be free; it is gravely mistaken; it is free only during the election of Members of Parliament; as soon as the Members are elected, the people is enslaved; it is nothing. In the brief moments of its freedom, the English people makes such a use of that freedom that it deserves to lose it.

The idea of representation is a modern one. It comes to us from feudal government, from that iniquitous and absurd system under which the human race is degraded and which dishonours the name of man. In the republics and even in the monarchies of the ancient world, the people never had representatives; the very word was unknown. It is remarkable in the case of Rome, where the tribunes were so sacred, that no one ever imagined that they might usurp the functions of the people; and in the midst of such a great multitude, they never attempted to pass on their own authority a single *plebiscitium.* One can judge, however, the embarrassment the crowd sometimes caused from what happened at the time of the Gracchi, when a great part of the citizens voted from the rooftops.

Where rights and freedom are everything, inconveniences are nothing. Among these wise people, everything was given its just measure; the lictors were allowed to do what the tribunes would not have dared to do; the people were not afraid that their lictors would wish to represent them.

To explain how, even so, the tribunes did represent the people, it is enough to consider how the government represents the sovereign. Since the law is nothing other than a declaration of the general will, it is clear that there cannot be representation of the people in the legislative power; but there may and should be such representation in the executive power, which is only the instrument for applying the law. This indicates that if we look carefully, we shall find that very few nations have laws. However that may be, it is certain that the tribunes, having no part of the executive power, could never represent the Roman people by the rights of their own office, but only by usurping those of the senate.

Among the Greeks, all that the people had to do, it did itself; it was continuously assembled in the market place. The Greek people lived in a mild climate; it was not at all avaricious; slaves did the work; its chief concern was its freedom. Without the same advantages, how can the same rights be preserved? Your harsher climate creates more necessities;* six months of the year the public places are uninhabitable; your muted tongues cannot make themselves heard in the open air; you care more for your profits than your freedom; and you fear slavery less than you fear poverty.

What? Is freedom to be maintained only with the support

* To adopt in cold countries the luxury and softness of the orientals is to ask to have their chains, to make submission even more inevitable than theirs.

of slavery? Perhaps. The two extremes meet. Everything outside nature has its disadvantages, civil society more than all the rest. There are some situations so unfortunate that one can preserve one's freedom only at the expense of the freedom of someone else; and the citizen can be perfectly free only if the slave is absolutely a slave. Such was the situation of Sparta. You peoples of the modern world, you have no slaves, but you are slaves yourselves; you pay for their liberty with your own. It is in vain that you boast of this preference; I see more cowardice than humanity in it.

I do not mean by all this to suggest that slaves are necessary or that the right of slavery is legitimate, for I have proved the contrary. I simply state the reasons why peoples of the modern world, believing themselves to be free, have representatives, and why peoples of the ancient world did not. However that may be, the moment a people adopts representatives it is no longer free; it no longer exists.

All things carefully considered, I do not see how it will be possible henceforth among people like us for the sovereign to maintain the exercise of its rights unless the republic is very small. But if it is very small, will it not be subjugated? No. I shall show later* how the external strength of a large people can be combined with the free government and good order of a small state.

CHAPTER 16

That the Institution of the Government is not a Contract

ONCE the legislative power is well established, it remains to establish similarly the executive power; for the latter, which operates only by particular acts, is essentially different from

---

* This is what I intended to do in the remaining part of this work, when, in dealing with foreign relations, I should have come to the subject of confederations. This subject is entirely new, and its principles have yet to be established.

the former, and is naturally separate from it. If it were possible for the sovereign, considered as such, to have the executive power, then the *de jure* and the *de facto* would be so confused that people would no longer know what was law and what was not; and the body politic, thus perverted, would soon fall prey to that very violence it was instituted to prevent.

The citizens being all equal by the social contract, all may prescribe what all must do, instead of nobody having a right to demand that another shall do what he does not do himself. For it is precisely this right, indispensable for giving life and movement to the body politic, that the sovereign gives to the prince in instituting the government.

Several theorists have claimed that this act of institution is a contract between the people and the magistrates it sets over itself, a contract which stipulates between the two parties the conditions under which the one undertakes to command and the other to obey. It will be admitted, I am sure, that this is a strange way of contracting. But let us see if the theory is tenable.

First, the supreme authority can no more be modified than it can be alienated; to limit it is to destroy it. It is absurd and self-contradictory that the sovereign should give itself a superior; to undertake to obey a master would be to return to absolute freedom.

Furthermore, it is clear that this contract of the people with such or such persons would be a particular act. From this it follows that this contract could not be a law, or an act of sovereignty, and hence that it would be illegitimate.

We see further that the contracting parties would, between themselves, be subject only to natural law, and so without any guarantee of their reciprocal commitments – and this is wholly repugnant to the civil state. Since the man who has force in his hand is always the master of what shall be done, this is like giving the name of 'contract' to the act of a man who says to another: 'I give you all my property on condition that you give me back what you please.'

There is only one contract in the state: that of the association itself, and this excludes all others. One cannot imagine any public contract that would not be a violation of the original contract.

CHAPTER 17

The Institution of the Government

IN what conceptual terms then should we think of the act by which the government is instituted? I shall explain first that this act is complex, or composed of two others, namely the establishment of the law and the execution of the law.

By the first, the sovereign enacts that there shall be a body of government established with such or such form; and it is clear that this act is a law.

By the second, the people names the magistrates who are to be invested with the government thus established. Since this nomination is a particular act, it is not a second law, but simply a sequel to the first and a function of government.

The difficulty is to understand how there can be an act of government before the government exists, and how the people, which is only sovereign or subject, can in certain circumstances become prince or magistrate.

Now it is here once more that the body politic reveals one of those astonishing properties by which it reconciles operations that seem to be contradictory. For this operation is accomplished by the sudden transformation of the sovereignty into democracy in such a way that without undergoing any visible change, and simply through a new relation of all to all, the citizens become magistrates and pass from general acts to particular acts, and from the law to its execution.

This change of relation is not a refinement of speculative

theory without example in practice; it happens every day in the English parliament, where the lower House on certain occasions transforms itself into a committee of the whole House the better to discuss affairs, and so becomes a simple committee of that sovereign court which it was itself a moment before; then later it reports to itself, in its capacity of House of Commons, on what it has just settled as a committee of the whole House, and again debates under one name what it has already decided under another.

It is the advantage peculiar to democratic government that it can be established in fact by a simple act of the general will. After this, the provisional government remains in office if such is the form adopted, or there is established in the name of the sovereign whatever government is prescribed by the law; and everything is then in order. It is not possible to institute the government in any other legitimate manner, without abandoning the principles established in earlier chapters.

CHAPTER 18

Means of Preventing the Usurpation of Government

FROM these explanations, it follows, in confirmation of Chapter 16, that the act which institutes the government is not a contract but a law, and that the holders of the executive power are not the people's masters but its officers; and that the people can appoint them and dismiss them as it pleases; and that there is no question of their contracting, but of obeying; and that in discharging the functions which the state imposes on them, they are only doing their duty as citizens, without having any sort of right to argue terms.

Thus when it happens that the people institutes a hereditary government, whether monarchical in one family, or aristocratic in a class of citizens, it does not enter into any undertaking; hereditary government is simply a provisional form that it gives to the administration until such time as it pleases to arrange it differently.

It is true that such changes are always dangerous, and that one should never touch an established government unless it has become incompatible with the public welfare; but such circumspection is a precept of politics and not a rule of law; and the state is no more bound to leave civil authority to its magistrates than military authority to its generals.

It is true again that in such cases one cannot observe with too great care all the formalities required to distinguish a regular and legitimate act from a seditious tumult, and the will of a whole people from the clamour of a faction. It is here above all that one must avoid yielding to socially harmful claims any more than is required by the strict application of the law; and it is from this obligation too that the prince derives a great opportunity of holding his power in defiance of the people, without it being possible to say that he has usurped it. For while appearing to exercise only his rights it is very easy for him to enlarge those rights and to prevent, on the pretext of public tranquillity, assemblies designed to re-establish good government; thus he exploits the silence which he prevents men breaking, and the irregularities which he makes them commit, to assume in his own favour the tacit consent of those whose mouths are closed by fear and to punish those who dare to speak. It was thus that the decemvirs, having been first elected for one year, and then continued for another, tried to retain their power in perpetuity, by no longer allowing the *comitia* to assemble. And it is by this simple means that all the governments of the world, once armed with the public force, sooner or later usurp the public authority.

The periodic assemblies of which I have already spoken are the right means to prevent or postpone this evil, above all those assemblies where no formal convocation is needed; for then the prince cannot prevent their meeting without openly proclaiming himself a violator of the laws and an enemy of the state.

At the opening of these assemblies, of which the only purpose is the maintenance of the social treaty, two motions should be put, motions which may never be annulled and which must be voted separately:

The first: 'Does it please the sovereign to maintain the present form of government?'

The second: 'Does it please the people to leave the administration to those at present charged with it?'

I assume here what I believe I have demonstrated, namely, that there is not in the state any fundamental law which may not be revoked, not even the social pact; for if all the citizens assemble to end this pact by a common accord, one cannot doubt that it is very legitimately ended. Grotius indeed thinks that each citizen may renounce his membership of the state, and recover his natural liberty and his goods on withdrawing from the country.* And it would be absurd if all the citizens united could not do what each of them separately can do.

---

* It being understood that none may leave the country to evade his duty, or avoid saving his country when it needs him. In such a case, flight would be criminal and punishable; it would not be withdrawal but desertion.

BOOK IV

CHAPTER I

That the General Will is Indestructible

So long as several men joined together consider themselves a single body, they have only one will, which is directed towards their common preservation and general well-being. Then all the animating forces of the state are vigorous and simple; its principles are clear and luminous; it has no incompatible or conflicting interests; the common good makes itself so manifestly evident that only common sense is needed to discern it. Peace, unity, equality are enemies of political sophistication. Upright and simple men are difficult to deceive precisely because of their simplicity; stratagems and clever arguments do not prevail upon them; they are not indeed subtle enough to be dupes. When we see among the happiest people in the world bands of peasants regulating the affairs of state under an oak tree, and always acting wisely, can we help feeling a certain contempt for the refinements of other nations, which employ so much skill and mystery to make themselves at once illustrious and wretched?

A state thus governed needs very few laws, and whenever there is a need to promulgate new ones, that need is universally seen. The first man to propose such a law is only giving voice to what everyone already feels, and there is no question either of intrigues or of eloquence to secure the enactment of what each has already resolved to do as soon as he is sure that all the others will do likewise.

What misleads theorists is that, as a result of looking only at states which are badly constituted from the beginning, they are struck by the impossibility of maintaining such a régime there. They laugh at the thought of all the follies that a clever knave or a sly orator could persuade the people of Paris or London to commit. They do not realize that Cromwell would have been put to forced labour by the people of Berne,* and the Duc de Beaufort imprisoned by the Genevese.†

However, when the social tie begins to slacken and the state to weaken, when particular interests begin to make themselves felt and sectional societies begin to exert an influence over the greater society, the common interest becomes corrupted and meets opponents; voting is no longer unanimous; the general will is no longer the will of all; contradictions and disputes arise; and even the best opinion is not allowed to prevail unchallenged.

In the end, when the state, on the brink of ruin, can maintain itself only in an empty and illusory form, when the social bond is broken in every heart, when the meanest interest impudently flaunts the sacred name of the public good, then the general will is silenced: everyone, animated by secret motives, ceases to speak as a citizen any more than as if the state had never existed; and the people enacts in the guise of laws iniquitous decrees which have private interests as their only end.

Does it follow from this that the general will is annihilated or corrupted? No, that is always unchanging, incorruptible and pure, but it is subordinated to other wills which prevail over it. Each man, in detaching his interest from the common interest, sees clearly that he cannot separate it entirely, but his share of the public good seems to him to be nothing compared to the exclusive good he seeks to make his own. Where his private good is not concerned, he wills the general good in his

* Literally 'belled'. It was the custom in Berne to hang bells round the necks of prisoners employed as forced labour on public works. [*Trans.*]

† Literally 'disciplined'. In Geneva *la discipline* was a prison for the intractable rogues of the town. See the Pléiade *Œuvres complètes de Jean-Jacques Rousseau*, vol. 3 p. 1491. [*Trans.*]

own interest as eagerly as anyone else. Even in selling his vote for money, he does not extinguish the general will in himself; he evades it. The fault he commits is to change the form of the question, and to answer something different from what is asked him; so that instead of saying, with his vote, 'It is advantageous to the state', he says, 'It is advantageous to this man or to that party that such or such a proposal should be adopted.' For this reason the sensible rule for regulating public assemblies is one intended not so much to uphold the general will there as to ensure that it is always questioned and always responds.

I might say a great deal here about the simple right of voting in every act of sovereignty, a right of which nothing can deprive citizens, and also about the right of speaking, proposing, dividing and debating – a right which the government always takes great care to assign only to its own members – but this important subject would require a separate treatise, and I cannot put everything in this one.

CHAPTER 2

The Suffrage

IT will be evident from what has been said in the preceding chapter that the manner in which public affairs are conducted gives a sufficiently accurate indication of the moral character and the state of health of the body politic. The greater harmony that reigns in the public assemblies, the more, in other words, that public opinion approaches unanimity, the more the general will is dominant; whereas long debates, dissensions and disturbances bespeak the ascendance of particular interests and the decline of the state.

This will seem less evident when two or several orders enter into the constitution, as in Rome with its patricians and plebeians, whose quarrels often disturbed the *comitia* even in the finest days of the Republic; but this exception to the rule is more apparent than real, for in Rome, as a result of an inherent defect in the body politic, there were, in a manner of speaking, two states in one, and what is not true of both together is true of each separately. And, indeed, even in the most tumultuous times, the plebiscites of the people always proceeded peacefully when the senate did not interfere, and votes were given with large majorities. The citizens having only one interest, the people had only one will.

At the other extreme of the cycle, unanimity reappears. This is when the citizens, lapsed into servitude, have no longer either freedom or will. Then fear and flattery change voting into acclamation; people no longer deliberate, they worship or they curse. Such was the shameful manner in which the senate gave voice to its opinions under the emperors. Sometimes it did so with absurd precautions. Tacitus mentions that under Otho, the senators covered Vitellius with execrations, but took care at the same time to make a deafening noise, so that Vitellius would not be able to distinguish what each one of them had said, lest he should ever by any chance become master.

These various considerations suggest the principles by which the counting of votes and the comparing of opinions should be arranged, depending on whether the general will is more or less easy to recognize, and on whether the state is more or less in decline.

There is only one law which by its nature requires unanimous assent. This is the social pact: for the civil association is the most voluntary act in the world; every man having been born free and master of himself, no one else may under any pretext whatever subject him without his consent. To assert that the son of a slave is born a slave is to assert that he is not born a man.

If, then, there are opposing voices at the time when the social pact is made, this opposition does not invalidate the contract; it merely excludes the dissentients; they are foreigners among the citizens. After the state is instituted, residence implies consent: to inhabit the territory is to submit to the sovereign.*

Apart from this original contract, the votes of the greatest number always bind the rest; and this is a consequence of the contract itself. Yet it may be asked how a man can be at once free and forced to conform to wills which are not his own. How can the opposing minority be both free and subject to laws to which they have not consented?

I answer that the question is badly formulated. The citizen consents to all the laws, even to those that are passed against his will, and even to those which punish him when he dares to break any one of them. The constant will of all the members of the state is the general will; it is through it that they are citizens and free.† When a law is proposed in the people's assembly, what is asked of them is not precisely whether they approve of the proposition or reject it, but whether it is in conformity with the general will which is theirs; each by giving his vote gives his opinion on this question, and the counting of votes yields a declaration of the general will. When, therefore, the opinion contrary to my own prevails, this proves only that I have made a mistake, and that what I believed to be the general will was not so. If my particular opinion had prevailed against the general will, I should have

* This should always be understood to refer only to free states, for elsewhere family, property, lack of asylum, necessity or violence may keep an inhabitant in the country unwillingly, and then his mere residence no longer implies consent either to the contract or to the violation of the contract.

† In Genoa the word *Libertas* may be seen on the doors of all the prisons and on the fetters of the galleys. This use of the motto is excellent and just. In fact, it is only the malefactors of all states who prevent the citizens from being free. In a country where all such people were in the galleys, the most perfect liberty would be enjoyed.

done something other than what I had willed, and then I should not have been free.

This presupposes, it is true, that all the characteristics of the general will are still to be found in the majority; when these cease to be there, no matter what position men adopt, there is no longer any freedom.

When I showed earlier in this essay how particular wills come to take the place of the general will in public deliberations, I made sufficiently clear what practical means may prevent that abuse, and I shall return to this subject later. As for the proportional number of votes required to declare the general will, I have also set forth the principles by which that number can be determined. A difference of a single vote destroys an equal division; a single opposing voice destroys unanimity; but between unanimity and an equal division there are numerous unequal divisions, and the desired proportion can be fixed at any of these points in accordance with the condition and on the needs of the body politic.

Two general maxims may serve to determine these ratios: the first, that the more important and serious the matter to be decided, the closer should the opinion which is to prevail approach unanimity; the second, the swifter the decision the question demands, the smaller the prescribed majority may be allowed to become; and in decisions which have to be given immediately, a majority of one must suffice. The first of these maxims might seem to be more suited to the enactment of laws, the second to the dispatch of administrative business. At all events, it is by a combination of the two maxims that we can determine the right size for the majority that is to decide on any question.

CHAPTER 3

Elections

ELECTIONS of the prince and magistrates, which are, as I have said, complex acts, can be arranged in two ways, by choice or by lot. Both means have been employed in different republics, and a very complicated mixture of the two can still be seen in the election of the Doge of Venice. 'Election by lot,' says Montesquieu, 'is natural to democracy.' I agree. But why is this so? 'Drawing lots,' he continues, 'is a method of election that wounds no one and gives every citizen a reasonable hope of serving his country.' But these are not good reasons.

If we remember that the election of chiefs is a function of government and not of sovereignty, we shall see why the method of lot is natural to democracy, where the administration is all the better in proportion as its acts are fewer.

In every true democracy, magistrature is not a privilege but a heavy responsibility, so that it cannot justly be imposed on one man rather than another. The law alone can impose this burden on the man to whom the lot falls. For in this case, since the conditions are equal for all and the choice does not depend on any human will, the universality of the law is not distorted by any particular application.

In an aristocracy the prince chooses the prince, the government perpetuates itself by its own actions; and then election by choice is appropriate.

The example of the election of the Doge of Venice, far from undermining this distinction, confirms it: such a mixed form suits a mixed government. It is a mistake to regard the government of Venice as a genuine aristocracy. For while the Venetian people has no part in the government, the Venetian nobility is itself a people. A multitude of poor Barnabites never comes near any magistrature, and its nobility rests on the empty title of Excellency and the right to attend the Great Council. And since this Great Council is as numerous as our General Council in Geneva, its illustrious members have no more privileges than our plain citizens. Hence there is no doubt that, apart from the extreme disparity between the two republics, the bourgeoisie of Geneva corresponds precisely to the patriciate of Venice; our natives and inhabitants correspond to the townsmen and the people of Venice, and our peasants to their subjects on the mainland; to sum up, from whatever point of view the Venetian Republic is considered, apart from its size, its government is no more aristocratic than our own. The whole difference lies in the fact that we have no head of state who holds office for life, and so we have not the same need for the method of election by lot.

Election by lot would have few disadvantages in a true democracy, for where all men were equal in character and talent as well as in principles and fortune, it would hardly matter who was chosen. But as I have already said, no true democracy exists.

When election by choice and election by lot are both employed, choice should be used to fill places that call for special skills, such as military commands, and lot for those where common sense, justice and integrity are enough, as in the case of political offices, for in a well constituted state, such qualities are found among all the citizens.

Under monarchical government, neither election by lot nor election by choice has any place. Since the monarch is by right the sole prince and only magistrate, the choice of his lieutenants belongs to him alone. When the Abbé de St Pierre proposed to increase the Councils of the King of France and have their members elected by ballot, he did not realize that he was proposing to change the form of government!

I have yet to speak of the method of voting and collecting

votes in the people's assembly, but perhaps the history of the Roman system would serve to demonstrate more forcefully all the principles that I might myself set forth. It will not be beneath the dignity of a thoughtful reader to consider in some detail how public and private business was conducted in an assembly of two hundred thousand men.

CHAPTER 4

The Roman Comitia

WE have no trustworthy records of the early history of Rome, and there is every likelihood that most of the tales we are told are fables;* indeed, in general, that most instructive part of the annals of peoples, which is the history of their institution, is the part we most lack. Experience teaches us daily the causes of revolutions in empires, but as peoples are no longer instituted, we have nothing better than conjecture to explain how they were once instituted.

The customs that we find established show at least that such customs must have had an origin. Traditions that recall these origins, that are supported by the best authorities, and confirmed by the best reasons, should pass for the most certain. Such are the principles I have tried to follow in enquiring how the freest and strongest people of the world exercised its supreme power.

After the foundation of Rome, the new-born Republic – that is, the founder's army, made up of Albans, Sabines and foreigners – was divided into three classes, which acquired by this division the name of *tribes*. Each of these tribes was further

* The name 'Rome', which is said to derive from *Romulus* is really Greek, and it means *force*; the name 'Numa' is also Greek, and it means *law*. Is it very probable that the first two kings of that city should have borne before they reigned names so clearly related to what they did?

divided into ten *curiae*, and each *curia* subdivided into *decuriae*, with chiefs named *curiones* and *decuriones* placed at their head.

In addition to this, there was drawn from each tribe a body of a hundred equites or knights, called a *century*, which indicates that these divisions, hardly necessary in a city, were in the first place purely military. But it seems that an instinct for greatness led this little town of Rome to provide itself from the outset with a system well suited to the capital of the world.

However, this original division soon had one disadvantageous consequence. The tribes of Albans* and Sabines† remained constant, while the tribe of foreigners‡ grew continuously as more foreigners were recruited, and it soon contained more members than the other two tribes combined. The remedy that Servius found for this dangerous fault was to alter the basis of the division, and in place of the racial distinction, which he abolished, he introduced one based on the district of the town occupied by each of the tribes. Instead of three tribes, he set up four, each occupying one of the hills of Rome and bearing its name. Thus he both corrected an existing inequality and forestalled any future inequality; and to ensure that the division should be one of men and not of places, he forbade the inhabitants of one district to move to another, and so prevented the races from merging together.

He also doubled the three original centuries of equites and added twelve new ones, but he let them keep their former names – a shrewd and simple means by which he succeeded in distinguishing the body of knights from that of the people without making the latter complain.

To these four urban tribes, Servius added fifteen others which were called rustic tribes, because they were formed of inhabitants of the country, arranged in so many cantons. Afterwards as many new tribes were formed, and the Roman

* Ramnenses.   † Tatientes.   ‡ Luceres.

people found itself divided into thirty-five tribes, a number which remained unchanged until the end of the Republic.

This distinction between tribes of the town and tribes of the country had one consequence worth noting since there is no other instance of it, and since Rome was indebted to it both for the preservation of her morals and for the growth of her empire. It might have been thought that the urban tribes would have soon monopolized the power and the honours and have been quick to diminish the standing of the rustic tribes. What happened was the contrary. The taste of the early Romans for a country life is well known. This taste came from their wise founder, who made freedom go together with rural labour and military service and, in a manner of speaking, relegated crafts, trades, intrigue, wealth and slavery to the city.

Since all the illustrious men in Rome thus lived in the country and cultivated the land, it became customary to look to the country for the mainstays of the Republic. And as this way of life was that of the most noble patricians, it was honoured by everyone; the simple and laborious life of villagers was preferred to the loose and idle life of the Roman bourgeois, and a man who would have been nothing but a miserable proletarian in the town became as a tiller of the soil a respected citizen. It was not without reason, says Varro, that our magnanimous ancestors established in the village the nursery of those robust and valiant men who defended them in time of war and nourished them in time of peace. Pliny states positively that the rustic tribes were honoured because of the men who belonged to them, and that whenever it was intended to degrade a coward, he was transferred in disgrace to one of the urban tribes. When Appius Claudius, the Sabine, came to set himself up in Rome, he was loaded with honours and inscribed as a member of a rustic tribe which afterwards took the name of his family. Finally, all the freed men joined the urban and never the rustic tribes, and throughout the Republic there was not a single example of any one of these freed men acceding to any magistrature, even though he had become a citizen.

This principle was excellent; but it was pushed so far that it finally produced an alteration, and certainly an abuse in the political system.

First, the censors, having long arrogated to themselves the right arbitrarily to transfer citizens from one tribe to another, allowed most men to enrol in the tribe of their choice, a concession which certainly did no good and which deprived the censorship of one of its great advantages. Moreover, the exalted and powerful men all had themselves enrolled in the rustic tribes, and the freed men remained with the common people in the urban tribes, so that the tribes generally ceased to have any local or territorial bases, and all were so muddled together that it was no longer possible to identify anyone without consulting the register; and this is why the word *tribe* came to have a personal instead of a territorial meaning, or rather came to be virtually fictitious.

It also came about that the urban tribes, being closer to the centre, often found themselves the strongest group in the *comitia*, and sold the state to such as deigned to buy the votes of the rabble who composed that assembly.

As for the *curiae*, since the founder had created ten in each tribe, the whole of the Roman people, at that time enclosed within the walls of the city, was composed of thirty *curiae*, each with its own temples, its Gods, its officials, its priests and its festivals called *compitalia*, which resembled the *Paganalia* later held by the rustic tribes.

When Servius introduced his new division, this number of thirty could not be divided equally between his four tribes, and he did not wish to alter it; in consequence, the *curiae*,

becoming independent of the tribes, formed another category
of inhabitants of Rome. But there was no question of *curiae* in
the rustic tribes or among the people who belonged to them;
for after the tribes had become a purely civil institution, and
another system introduced for the levying of troops, the
military divisions of Romulus proved superfluous. Thus,
although each citizen was enrolled in a tribe, there were many
who were not members of a *curia*.

Servius made yet a third division, which had nothing to do
with the first two, and which became by reason of its consequences the most important of all. He distributed the whole
Roman people into six classes, arranged neither on a personal
nor on a residential basis, but according to wealth; so that the
first classes were filled with the rich, the last with the poor,
and the intermediate classes with men of moderate fortunes.
These six classes were subdivided into 193 other bodies called
centuries, and these bodies were so distributed that the first
class accounted for more than half of them, and the last class
for a single one only. Thus it came about that the class with
the fewest number of men had the greatest number of centuries, while the last whole class counted only as one single
subdivision, although it contained more than half the inhabitants of Rome.

In order that the people should less well perceive the consequences of this division, Servius disguised it in a military
form; he put into the second class two centuries of ar-
mourers and into the fourth class two centuries of weapon-
makers. In each class, except the last, he differentiated between
young and old, that is to say, between those liable to bear
arms and those legally exempt on grounds of age; and this
distinction, more than that of wealth, made it necessary to
hold frequent censuses. Finally he prescribed that the assembly
should be held in the Campus Martius, and that all those of
military age should attend bearing arms.

The reason he did not make the same differentiation between young and old in the last class is simply that the common people who belonged to it did not have the honour of bearing arms in the service of their country; only those who owned hearths had the right to defend them. Among the countless hordes of beggars who ornament the armies of kings today there is perhaps none who would not have been expelled with disdain from a Roman cohort in the days when soldiers were the defenders of liberty.

In the last class, however, a distinction was made between *proletarians* and those who were called *capite censi*. The former, not wholly reduced to nothing, at least gave citizens to the state, even sometimes soldiers in times of pressing need. But those who possessed nothing whatever, and could be reckoned only by the counting of heads, were considered altogether null, and Marius was the first who condescended to enrol them.

Without deciding here whether this third classification was good or bad in itself, one can, I think, safely say that it was practicable only because of the simple habits of the early Romans, their taste for agriculture, and their contempt alike for commerce and for the pursuit of profit. Where is the modern people, whose devouring greed, unsettled hearts, intrigue, continual movement and constant reversals of fortune would have allowed such a system to last for twenty years without overturning the whole state? It should also be remembered that the morals of the Roman people and the office of censorship had the strength to correct the evils of this system, and that a rich man could find himself relegated to the class of the poor for making too ostentatious a display of his wealth.

From all this it is easy to understand why more than five Roman classes are hardly ever mentioned, even though there were actually six. The sixth, which provided neither soldiers for the army nor voters for the Campus Martius* and had therefore virtually no function in the Republic, was seldom given any thought.

Such were the different divisions of the Roman people. Let us now consider the effect the divisions had in the assemblies. The assemblies which were lawfully convened were called *comitia*, and generally met in the Roman forum or in the Campus Martius; they were distinguished as *comitia curiata*, *comitia centuriata* and *comitia tributa*, according to which form was employed. The *comitia curiata* was founded by Romulus, the *comitia centuriata* by Servius, and the *comitia tributa* originated in the tribunes of the people. No law was sanctioned and no magistrate elected except in the *comitia*, and as there was no citizen who was not enrolled in a *curia*, century or tribe, it follows that no citizen was excluded from the right to vote, and that the Roman people was truly sovereign, both in law and in fact.

For the *comitia* to be legally convened and for its decisions to have the force of law, three conditions had to be observed: first, the body or the magistrate convening the assembly had to be vested with the necessary authority; secondly, the assembly had to be held on one of the days permitted by law; thirdly, the auguries had to be favourable.

The reason for the first of these rules needs no explanation. The second was a matter of policy; the assembly was not allowed to meet on holidays or market days, because the country people, who came to Rome to do business, did not have time to spend the day in the forum. The third rule enabled the Senate to keep a restraining hand on a proud and

---

* I say 'Campus Martius' because this was where the *comitia centuriata* met. In the other two forms of assembly, the people met in the forum or elsewhere, and then the *capite censi* had as much influence and authority as the leading citizens.

restless people and temper the ardour of seditious tribunes – although the latter found more than one way of evading this check.

Laws and the election of chiefs were not the only matters submitted to the judgement of the *comitia*. Since the Roman people had usurped the most important functions of government, one could say that the fate of Europe was determined in those assemblies. The variety of public business explains the several forms which the *comitia* took, according to the matters which had to be decided.

To judge these various forms it is necessary only to compare them. Romulus, in establishing the *curiae* aimed to balance the Senate against the people and balance the people against the Senate, while himself dominating both alike. Under this arrangement he gave the people all the authority of numbers to balance the authority of power and wealth which he left to the patricians. But true to the spirit of monarchy, he nevertheless gave the great advantage to the patricians, in that they could buy clients to influence numerical majorities. This admirable institution of patrons and clients was a masterpiece of politics and humanity, without which the patriciate, so contrary to the spirit of the Republic, could not have survived. To Rome alone belongs the honour of giving the world this noble example, from which no abuse has ever come, but which has never been followed elsewhere.

This same form of *curiae* continued under the kings up to Servius, and as the reign of the last of the Tarquins was not held to be legitimate, the royal laws were generally known by the name of *leges curiatae*.

Under the Republic, the *curiae*, which were still limited to the four urban tribes, and still included only the population of Rome, pleased neither the Senate, which led the patricians, nor the tribunes who, in spite of being plebeian, led the more moneyed citizens. Thus the *curiae* fell into discredit, fell so low indeed that their thirty lictors met to do what the *comitia curiae* should have done.

The division into centuries was so favourable to the aristocracy that it is not at first easy to see why the Senate did not always carry the day in the *comitia* which bore that name, and by which the consuls, censors and other cural magistrates were elected. For indeed, of the 193 centuries which formed the six classes of the entire Roman people, the first class contained 98, and since votes were counted by centuries only, this first class had a majority over all the others. When all these centuries were in agreement, the rest of the votes were not even counted; and what had been decided by a minority passed for a decision of the multitude; so it can be said that in the centuriate assemblies matters were decided by majorities of money rather than of votes.

But this excessive power was tempered in two ways. First, the tribunes ordinarily, and a large number of plebeians always, were in a class with the rich, and balanced the influence of the patricians in the first class.

Secondly, the centuries were not always summoned to vote in their order or rank, which would have meant beginning with the first class; instead, a century was chosen by lot* and that century alone went on to elect, after which the other centuries were convened on a different day by order of rank to repeat the election, and generally they confirmed it. Thus the authority of example was taken away from rank and given to chance, according to the principle of democracy.

This custom had yet another advantage; it meant that the citizens from the country had time between the elections to inform themselves of the merits of the candidates provisionally nominated, and therefore did not vote in ignorance. But under

---

* The century thus drawn was called *praerogativa* because it was the first required to cast its vote; and this is the origin of our word 'prerogative'.

the pretext of speeding up procedure this custom was finally abolished, and both elections were held on the same day.

The *comitia tributa* was, strictly speaking, the council of the Roman people. It could be convened only by the tribunes; it was the assembly where the tribunes were elected and it was there that they passed their plebiscites. Not only had the Senate no status in the assembly, but no senator had even the right to attend, and being thus forced to submit to laws in the enactment of which they had no voice, the senators were to that extent less free than the humblest citizen. This injustice was altogether ill conceived, and alone sufficed to invalidate the decrees of a body to which all its members were not admitted. Had all the patricians attended the *comitia*, according to their rights as citizens, they would not, as simple individuals, have had any great influence on a vote taken by enumerating heads, and in which the humblest proletarian would count for as much as the prince of the Senate.

Thus, it will be seen that besides the order which emerged from the various systems of collecting the votes of so vast a people, these several methods were not in themselves insignificant, but that each had effects connected with the opinions that led to its being chosen.

Without going further into long details, it emerges from the explanation already given, that the *comitia tributa* was the assembly most favourable to popular government and the *comitia centuriata* to aristocracy. In the case of the *comitia curiata*, where the populace of Rome alone formed the majority, their tendency to favour tyranny and evil designs led them to fall into disrepute, so that even the seditious elements avoided these assemblies lest their presence should arouse suspicion concerning their conspiracies. There is no doubt that the whole majesty of the Roman people was to be seen only in the *comitia centuriata*; this alone was a full assembly, for the *comitia curiata* excluded the rustic tribes and the *comitia tributa* excluded the Senate and patricians.

The system of voting used by the Romans was as simple as were their manners and morals, if less simple than that of Sparta. Each man gave his vote by word of mouth, and a clerk recorded it; the majority of individual votes in each tribe determined the decision of that tribe, the majority of tribal votes the decision of the people; and the same thing was done in the *curiae* and *centuriae*. This was a good method so long as honesty prevailed among the citizens and everyone was ashamed to give his vote to an unjust cause or an unworthy candidate. But when the people grew corrupt and votes were bought, it became expedient for the ballot to be cast in secret, so that the buyers of votes might be restrained by mistrust of the sellers, and scoundrels given the chance of not being traitors also.

I am aware that Cicero condemns this change of method, and holds it partly responsible for the ruin of the Republic. But while I am mindful of the weight which the authority of Cicero ought to bear, I do not agree with him. On the contrary, I think that it was by having too few such changes that the ruin of the state was accelerated. For just as the diet of healthy people is unsuited to the sick, so one should not try to give to a corrupt people the same laws as those which suit a virtuous people. Nothing does more to bear out this principle than the long life of the Republic of Venice, which still retains a simulacrum of existence solely because its laws are uniquely suited to wicked men.

Now the Roman citizens had tablets distributed among them, so that each might cast his vote without anyone's knowing his opinion. New arrangements were also devised for the collection of tablets, the counting of votes, the comparison of numbers, and so forth. This did not prevent the officers*

---

* *Custodes, Diribitores, Rogatores suffragiorum.*

entrusted with these functions from being suspected of dishonesty. Finally, edicts designed to prevent intrigue and the buying and selling of votes were passed in such numbers that their very multiplicity proclaims their ineffectiveness.

Towards the last years of the Republic, the Romans were often forced to resort to extraordinary expedients to make up for the inadequacy of the law. Sometimes miracles were invoked, but this device, if it could impose on the people, did not impose on those who ruled them. Sometimes assemblies were hurriedly convened, before candidates had time to pay out their bribes; sometimes a whole session was taken up with filibustering, when it was seen that the people had been seduced and was about to make a wrong decision. But ambition in the end overcame all obstacles; and the most incredible fact of all is that so numerous a people, in the midst of so many abuses, still continued, thanks to its ancient rules of order, to elect magistrates, to enact laws, to judge cases and to conduct private and public business with almost as much facility as the Senate itself might have commanded.

CHAPTER 5

The Tribunate

WHEN it is impossible to settle an exact balance between the constitutive parts of the state, or when causes beyond control go on altering the relations between them, then a special magistrate is established, as a body separate from the other magistrates, to put every element in its right balance and to serve as a link or middle term, either between the prince and the people or between the prince and the sovereign, or alternatively, between both at the same time if that is necessary.

This body, which I shall call the *tribunate*, is the guardian of the laws and of the legislative power. It serves sometimes to protect the sovereign against the government, as did the tribunes of the people in Rome, sometimes to uphold the government against the people, as does the Council of Ten today in Venice, and sometimes to keep a balance between the two, as did the Ephors of Sparta.

The tribunate is not a constitutive part of the republic, and it ought to have no share of either the legislative or executive power, but for this very reason its own power is all the greater, for although it can do nothing, it can prevent anything from being done. As the defender of the laws, it is more sacred and more venerated than the prince who executes laws or the sovereign which legislates. This is very clearly shown in the case of Rome, where the proud patricians, who always despised the people as a whole, were forced to bow before an ordinary officer of the people who wielded neither sacred nor legal authority.

A wisely tempered tribunate is the strongest buttress of a good constitution, but if it has the least degree of power beyond what is necessary, it will overthrow everything. It is not by its nature prone to weakness, and if it is anything at all, it will never be less than it ought to be.

It degenerates into tyranny when it usurps the executive power of which it is only the moderator, and when it tries to make the laws it ought only to protect. The enormous power of the Ephors, which represented no danger so long as Sparta preserved its morale, sped corruption once corruption began. The blood of Agis shed by the tyrants was avenged by his successor; the crimes and the punishments of the Ephors equally hastened the collapse of the Republic, and after Cleomenes, Sparta was nothing. Rome perished in the same way, and the excessive power which the tribunes usurped by degrees finally served, with the aid of laws made to defend liberty, to protect the very emperors who destroyed liberty. As for the

Council of Ten in Venice, it is a tribunal of blood, which is baneful as much to the patricians as to the people, and which, far from giving supreme protection to the law, serves only, now that the law has been debased, for the striking of stealthy blows that none dare look upon.

A tribunate, like a government, is weakened by the multiplication of its members. When the tribunes of the Roman people, originally two, then five, sought to double their number, the Senate gave its consent, confident of using one part to check the others; and this it did not fail to effect.

The best method of preventing the usurpations of such a formidable body – though it is a method which no government has ever yet employed – would be not to make the tribunate permanent but to prescribe the intervals during which it should remain suspended. These intervals, which should not be so great as to give abuses time to take root, could be specified by law in such a manner that in case of need they might be shortened by an extraordinary commission.

This method appears to me to have no disadvantages, for since, as I have said, the tribunate is in no sense a part of the constitution, it can be removed without detriment to it; this also seems to me an efficacious method, since a newly established magistrate would not enter office with the power that his predecessors had, but only with that given him by law.

CHAPTER 6

Dictatorship

THE inflexibility of the laws, which prevents them from bending to circumstances, may in certain cases make them injurious, and bring about in a time of crisis the ruin of the state. The ordered and slow procedures of legal formalities require a measure of time that circumstances do not always afford. There may be a thousand eventualities which the lawgiver has not foreseen, and it is a very necessary part of foresight to know that one cannot foresee everything.

For this reason, one should not seek to make political institutions so rigid that one is deprived of the power to suspend their operation. Even Sparta allowed its laws at times to lie dormant.

But it is only the greatest emergency that can counterweigh the dangers of tampering with the public order; and the sacred power of the laws should never be suspended except when the safety of the fatherland is at stake. In these rare and obvious cases, the public security is provided for by a special act making that security the responsibility of the person who is most worthy. This responsibility may be assigned in two ways, according to the nature of the emergency.

If increasing the activity of the government is adequate to counteract the danger, then this activity should be concentrated in the hands of one or two members of the government. In this case, it is not the authority of the laws which is being diminished, but only the form of the administration. But if the danger is such that the apparatus of law is itself an obstacle to safety, then a supreme head must be nominated with power to silence all the laws and temporarily suspend the sovereign authority. In such a case the general will is indubitable; for it is clear that the prime concern of the people is that the state shall not perish. Thus the suspension of the legislative authority does not abolish it; the magistrate who silences it cannot make it speak; he dominates it, without having the power to represent it; he can do everything, except make laws.

The first of these two methods was used by the Roman Senate when, according to a hallowed formula, it entrusted the consuls with the safety of the Republic; the second was used when one of the two consuls nominated a dictator* – a device that Rome had learned from Alba.

At the beginning of the Republic, the Romans often resorted to dictatorship, because conditions were not yet sufficiently settled for the state to maintain itself by the strength of its constitution. The people's moral character made unnecessary at that time many of the precautions which might have been needed at other times, so men did not fear that a dictator would abuse his position or that he would attempt to prolong his office beyond its term. It seemed, on the contrary, that so much power was a burden to those who wielded it; for they hastened to divest themselves of it, as if standing in the place of the laws made it altogether too onerous and perilous an office.

So it is not because there was a danger of its being abused, but because there was a danger of its being degraded that one condemns the imprudent employment of this supreme magistrature in the early days of the Republic. For while it was wasted on elections, dedications and purely formal things, there was reason to fear that it would become less forceful when it was really needed, and that the people would come to regard dictatorship as an empty title used only to give dignity to idle ceremonies.

Towards the end of the Republic, the Romans, becoming more circumspect, were as sparing in their use of dictatorship as they had once been prodigal, and with as little reason. It was easy to see that their fears were ill founded, and that the weakness of the capital was at that time its protection against the magistrates it had in its midst, that a dictator could in certain cases defend the public freedom without ever being able to invade it, and that the fetters of Rome were not forged in Rome itself, but in the Roman armies; the weak resistance that Marius offered Sulla, and Pompey Caesar, showed plainly what could

* This nomination took place by night and in secret, as if they were ashamed to put a man above the law.

be expected of internal authority faced with external force.

This mistake led the Romans to commit great wrongs. There was, for example, their failure to nominate a dictator in the Catilina affair; for since this was a matter which concerned only the city itself, or at most a few Italian provinces, the unlimited authority which the law gave a dictator would have facilitated the ready crushing of that conspiracy, which was in fact suppressed only by a concurrence of lucky accidents, such as human prudence could never have expected.

Instead of naming a dictator, the Senate was content to transmit all its powers to the consuls, as a result of which Cicero, in order to act effectively, was obliged to exceed his powers on a crucial point; and though, in a first transport of joy, the Romans approved of his conduct, it was not without justice that he was afterwards asked to account for the blood of citizens shed in violation of the laws – a reproach which could not have been addressed to a dictator. But the consul's eloquence carried everything before him, and he himself, though a Roman, loved his own glory better than his country; and instead of seeking a lawful and certain means of serving the state, he sought all the honour of the affair for himself.* Thus he was justly honoured as the liberator of Rome, and no less justly punished as the violator of Roman laws. However splendid his recall from exile may have been, it was undoubtedly an act of pardon.

For the rest, in whatever manner this important commission of dictatorship is conferred, it is imperative to limit its duration to one short term that can never be prolonged; in the emergencies which call for its institution, the state is soon lost or saved, and once the urgent need is over, dictatorship becomes either tyrannical or useless. In Rome, where the term was of

---

* He could not have been sure of this if he had proposed appointing a dictator, for he did not dare to name himself, and he could not be sure that his colleagues would name him.

six months, most of the dictators abdicated before that time had expired. If the term had been longer, they might have been tempted to prolong it still further, like the decemvirs, who held office for a year. The dictator, having only the time to meet the need which had prompted his appointment, had none in which to meditate on further projects.

CHAPTER 7

The Censorial Tribunal

JUST as the general will is declared by the law, so is the public judgement declared by the censorial office; public opinion is that form of law of which the censor is the minister, and which he, on the model of the prince, merely applies to particular cases.

Far, then, from the censorial tribunal being the arbiter of the people's opinion, it is only the spokesman; and as soon as it departs from this, its decisions are void and without effect.

It is useless to separate the morals of a nation from the objects of its esteem; for both spring from the same principle and both necessarily merge together. Among all the peoples of the world, it is not nature but opinion which governs the choice of their pleasures. Reform the opinions of men, and their morals will be purified of themselves. Men always love what is good or what they think is good, but it is in their judgement that they err; hence it is their judgement that has to be regulated. To judge morals is to judge what is honoured; to judge what is honoured, is to look to opinion as law.

The opinions of a people spring from its constitution; although the law does not regulate morals, it is legislation that gives birth to morals; when legislation weakens, morals degenerate; and then the rulings of the censors will not accomplish what the law has failed to achieve.

From this it follows that the censorial office may be useful in preserving morals, but never in restoring morals. Set up censors while the laws are still vigorous; for as soon as the vigour is lost, everything is hopeless; nothing legitimate has any force once the laws have force no longer.

The censorial office sustains morals by preventing opinions from being corrupted, by preserving their integrity with wise rulings, and sometimes even by settling points on which opinion is uncertain. The use of seconds in duels, carried to an impassioned extreme in the kingdom of France, was abolished by a single edict of the King: 'as for those who are cowardly enough to name seconds'. This judgement anticipated that of the public, and settled it with one stroke. But when the same edicts sought to declare that it was cowardice also to fight duels – which is very true, but at variance with popular opinion – the public scoffed at this decision on a matter about which its mind was made up.

I have said elsewhere* that since public opinion is not subject to constraint, there should be no vestige of constraint in the tribunal established to represent it. We cannot too greatly admire the skill with which this device, entirely alien to the moderns, was put into effect by the Romans and even by the Lacedaemonians.

Once when a man of bad character put forward a good idea in the council of Sparta, the Ephors, ignoring him, had the same thing proposed by a virtuous citizen. What an honour for the one, what a disgrace for the other; yet neither praise nor blame was given to either. Certain drunkards from Samos†

* In this chapter I have only indicated what I have already discussed at great length in my *Lettre à d'Alembert*.

† They were actually from another island, but delicacy of language forbids me to name it here. [Note added in Edition of 1782. In a manuscript note, Rousseau explained 'They were of Chios, and not of Samos, but in view of the subject matter I did not dare use that word in the text.' In French the word *'Chio'*, the Greek root of the modern French verb *chier* (to shit), was 'not in decent use'. *Trans.*]

once defiled the tribunal of the Ephors; the following day the Samians were given permission by public edict to be filthy. An actual punishment would have been less severe than such a form of impunity. When Sparta has pronounced on what is and what is not decent, Greece does not dispute its judgements.

CHAPTER 8

The Civil Religion

A T first men had no kings but the Gods, and their only government was theocratic. They reasoned like Caligula, and in the circumstances they reasoned rightly. A prolonged debasement of feelings and ideas was needed before man could make up his mind to accept one of his own kind as master, and to persuade himself that in doing so he had done well.

From this single fact, that a God was placed at the head of every political society, it follows that there were as many Gods as peoples. Two peoples alien to one another, and nearly always enemies, could not long recognize the same master: two armies going into battle could not obey the same commander. Thus national divisions produced polytheism, and this in turn produced religious and civil intolerance, which are naturally the same, as I shall explain later.

The fanciful idea of the Greeks that they had rediscovered their own Gods being worshipped by barbarian peoples originated in the Greek habit of regarding themselves as the natural sovereigns of those same peoples. But in our own times, it is a ludicrous parody of learning which studies the identity of the Gods of different nations, as if Moloch, Saturn and Chronos could be the same God, as if the Baal of the Phoenicians, the Zeus of the Greeks, and the Jupiter of the Romans could be identical; as if there could be anything in common between chimerical beings with different names!

But if it is asked why under paganism, when each state had its own religious cult and its own Gods, there were no wars of religion, I answer that it was due to this very fact that each state, having its own faith as well as its own government, did not distinguish between its Gods and its laws. Political war was just as much theological war; the provinces of the Gods were determined, so to speak, by the frontiers of nations. The God of one people had no rights over other peoples. The Gods of the Pagans were in no sense jealous Gods; they divided the empire of the world between them; even Moses and the Hebrew people sometimes countenanced this idea by speaking of the God of Israel. It is true that they did not recognize the Gods of the Canaanites, a proscribed people who were doomed to destruction, and whose country they were to occupy; but consider how they spoke of the divinities of neighbouring peoples, whom they were forbidden to attack: 'Is not the possession of that which belongs to Chamos your God lawfully your due?' says Jephthah to the Ammonites. 'By the same title we possess the lands which our conquering God has taken.'*

But when the Jews, subject to the Kings of Babylon, and afterwards to the Kings of Syria, stubbornly sought to recognize no other God but their own, this refusal was regarded as a rebellion against their conquerors, and it brought on the Jews those persecutions of which we read in their history, and of which we find no other example before the coming of Christianity.†

* *Nonne ea quae possidet Chamos deus tuus, tibi jure debentur?* Such is the text of the Vulgate. Father de Carrières translates it thus:'Do you not believe that you have a right to possess that which belongs to your God Chamos?' I do not know the bearing of the Hebrew text, but I notice that in the Vulgate, Jephthah positively recognizes the rights of the God Chamos, and that the French translation weakens this recognition by adding an 'according to you' which is not in the Latin.

† It is clear beyond dispute that the Phocian war, called the Holy War, was not a war of religion. Its object was to punish sacrilege, and not to make unbelievers submit.

Since each religion was thus attached exclusively to the laws of the state which prescribed it, and since there was no means of converting people except by subduing them, the only missionaries were conquerors; and since the obligation to change faith was part of the law of conquest, it was necessary to conquer before preaching conversion. Far from men fighting for the Gods, it was, as in Homer, the Gods who fought for men; each people asked its own God for victory, and paid for it with new altars. The Romans, before taking a town, called upon its Gods to abandon it; when they allowed the Tarentines to keep their angry Gods, it was in the belief that those Gods were subject to their own and obliged to pay them homage. They let the vanquished keep their own Gods just as they let them keep their own laws. A crown dedicated to Jupiter of the Capitol was often the only tribute they exacted.

In the end, when the Romans had spread their faith and their Gods with their empire, and often themselves adopted those of the vanquished in giving one or the other the rights of citizenship, the peoples of this vast empire gradually found themselves with a multitude of Gods and faiths, which were everywhere almost the same; and this is how paganism became one and the same religion throughout the known world.

It was in these circumstances that Jesus came to establish a spiritual kingdom on earth; this kingdom, by separating the theological system from the political, meant that the state ceased to be a unity, and it caused those intestine divisions which have never ceased to disturb Christian peoples. Now as this new idea of a kingdom of another world could never have entered the minds of pagans, they always regarded the Christians as true rebels who, under the cloak of hypocritical submission, only awaited the moment to make themselves independent and supreme, and cunningly to usurp that authority which they made a show of respecting while they were weak. Such was the cause of the persecutions.

What the pagans feared did indeed happen; then everything altered its countenance; the humble Christians changed their tune and soon the so-called kingdom of the other world was seen to become, under a visible ruler, the most violent despotism of this world.

However, since princes and civil laws have always existed, the consequence of this dual power has been an endless conflict of jurisdiction, which has made any kind of good polity impossible in Christian states, where men have never known whether they ought to obey the civil ruler or the priest.

Many peoples, even in Europe or nearby, have tried to preserve or re-establish the ancient system, but without success: the spirit of Christianity has won completely. The religious cult has always kept, or recovered, its independence of the sovereign, and has lacked its necessary connexion with the state. Mahomet had very sound opinions, taking care to give unity to his political system, and for as long as the form of his government endured under the caliphs who succeeded him, the government was undivided and, to that extent, good. But the Arabs, in becoming prosperous, cultured, polished, effeminate and soft, were subjugated by the barbarians; then the division between the two powers was started afresh, and even though the division is less apparent among the Moslems than among the Christians, it nevertheless exists, above all in the sect of Ali and in states like Persia where it has never ceased to make itself felt.

Among us, the Kings of England have established themselves as heads of the church and the Czars have done the same. But with this title they have made themselves not so much masters as ministers, and have acquired not so much the right to change the church as the power to preserve it; they are not legislators, they are only princes. Wherever the clergy constitutes a body,* it is master and legislator in its own house. Thus there are two powers, two sovereigns, in England and in Russia, just as there are elsewhere.

Of all Christian authors, the philosopher Hobbes is the only one who saw clearly both the evil and the remedy, and who dared to propose reuniting the two heads of the eagle and fully restoring that political unity without which neither the state nor the government will ever be well constituted. But he should have seen that the dominant spirit of Christianity was incompatible with his system, and that the interest of the prince will always be stronger than that of the state. It is not so much the horrible and false parts of Hobbes's system that have made it hated, but the parts which are just and true.†

I believe that if the historical facts were analysed from this point of view, we could easily refute the opposing beliefs of both Bayle and Warburton, the one holding that no religion is useful to the body politic, the other that Christianity is its best support. We could refute the first by showing that no state has ever been founded without religion as its base; and we could refute the second by showing that the Christian law is at bottom more injurious than serviceable to a robust constitution of the state. For this to be clearly understood, I think I have only to give a little more precision to the

---

* It should be noted that it is not so much the formal assemblies, like those of France, which bind the clergy together in a body, but rather the communion of churches. Communion and excommunication are the social compact of the clergy, one through which they will always be masters of both peoples and kings. All the priests who communicate together are fellow citizens, even though they are at opposite ends of the earth. This invention is a masterpiece of politics. There was nothing like it among the pagan priests; hence they never constituted a body of clergy.

† See, among other things, in a letter of Grotius to his brother dated 11 April 1643, what that learned man approved of and what he disapproved of in Hobbes's *De Cive*. It is true that, being inclined to indulgence, he forgives that author the bad for the sake of the good, but not everyone is so merciful.

exceedingly vague idea of religion, as it bears upon my subject.

Religion, considered in connexion with societies, whether general or particular, can be divided into two categories, the religion of the man and the religion of the citizen. The first, without temples, altars or rituals, and limited to inward devotion to the supreme God and the eternal obligations of morality, is the pure and simple religion of the Gospel, the true theism, and might be called the divine natural law. The religion of the citizen is the religion established in a single country; it gives that country its Gods and its special tutelary deities; it has its dogmas, its rituals, its external forms of worship laid down by law; and to the one nation which practises this religion, everything outside is infidel, alien, barbarous; and it extends the rights and duties of man only so far as it extends its altars. Such were the religions of all the early peoples; and we might give it the name of civil or positive divine law.

There is a third and more curious kind of religion, which gives men two legislative orders, two rulers, two homelands, puts them under two contradictory obligations, and prevents their being at the same time both churchmen and citizens. Such is the religion of the Lamas, such is that of the Japanese, and such is Catholic Christianity. One might call this the religion of the priest. It produces a kind of mixed and anti-social system of law which has no name.

From the political point of view, each of these three kinds of religion has its defects. The third kind is so manifestly bad that the pleasure of demonstrating its badness would be a waste of time. Everything that destroys social unity is worthless; and all institutions that set man at odds with himself are worthless.

The second kind of religion is good in that it joins divine worship to a love of the law, and that in making the home-land the object of the citizens' adoration, it teaches them that the service of the state is the service of the tutelary God. This is a kind of theocracy, in which there can be no pontiff other than the prince, and no priests except the magistrates. Then to die for one's country is to become a martyr, to break the law to be impious, and to subject a guilty man to public execration is to hand him over to the wrath of God: *sacer esto.*

But this kind of religion is also bad; since it is based on error and lies, it deceives men, and makes them credulous and superstitious; it buries the true worship of God in empty ceremonials. It is bad, again, when it becomes exclusive and tyrannical, and makes a people bloodthirsty and intolerant, so that men breathe only murder and massacre, and believe they are doing a holy deed in killing those who do not accept their Gods. This puts the people concerned into a natural state of war with all others, and this is something destructive of its own security.

There remains the religion of the private person, or Christianity, not the Christianity of today, but that of the Gospel, which is altogether different. Under this holy, sublime and true religion, men, as children of the same God, look on all others as brothers, and the society which unites them is not even dissolved by death.

But this religion, having no specific connexion with the body politic, leaves the law with only the force the law itself possesses, adding nothing to it; and hence one of the chief bonds necessary for holding any particular society together is lacking. Nor is this all: for far from attaching the hearts of the citizens to the state, this religion detaches them from it as from all other things of this world; and I know of nothing more contrary to the social spirit.

It is said that a people of true Christians would form the most perfect society imaginable. I see but one great flaw in this hypothesis, namely that a society of true Christians would not be a society of men.

I would say, too, that this imagined society, for all its perfection, would be neither the strongest nor the most durable. Being perfect, it would be without bonds of union; its ruinous defect would lie in its very perfection.

Everyone would do his duty; the people would obey the law; the rulers would be just and moderate; the magistrates would be honest and incorruptible; the soldiers would scorn death; there would be neither vanity nor luxury. But let us look further.

Christianity is a wholly spiritual religion, concerned solely with the things of heaven; the Christian's homeland is not of this world. The Christian does his duty, it is true, but he does it with profound indifference towards the good or ill success of his deeds. Provided that he has nothing to reproach himself for, it does not matter to him whether all goes well or badly here on earth. If the state prospers, he hardly dares to enjoy the public happiness; he fears lest he become proud of his country's glory; if the state perishes, he blesses the hand of God that weighs heavily on His people.

For such a society to be peaceful and for harmony to prevail, every citizen without exception would have to be an equally good Christian. If, unhappily, there should appear one ambitious man, one hypocrite, one Catilina, for example, or one Cromwell among them, that man would readily trample over his pious compatriots. Christian charity does not allow us readily to think ill of our neighbours. When a man is cunning enough to master the art of imposing on others, and gains a part of the public authority, there, behold, is a man of established dignity; and God wills that he be respected; soon, we see a man of power, and God wills that he be obeyed. Suppose he abuses the power of which he is the depositary? Then he is the scourge with which God chastises his children. Christians would have scruples about expelling the usurper; for that would mean disturbing the public peace, using violence, shedding blood, and all this accords ill with Christian mildness. And after all what does it matter whether one is free or a slave in this vale of tears? The essential thing is to go to paradise, and resignation is but one more means to that end.

Suppose a foreign war breaks out. The citizens will march without reluctance to war; no one among them will think of flight; all will do their duty – but they will do it without passion for victory; they know better how to die than to conquer. It does not matter to them whether they are victors or vanquished. Does not providence know better than they what is needful? One can imagine what advantage a proud, impetuous and passionate enemy would draw from their stoicism. Set them at war against a generous people whose hearts are devoured by an ardent love of glory and their country; imagine your Christian republic confronted by Sparta or Rome, and your pious Christians will be beaten, crushed, destroyed before they have time to collect their wits, or they will owe their salvation only to the contempt which their enemy feels for them.

I myself think it was an excellent oath that was taken by the soldiers of Fabius; they did not swear to conquer or die, but to return as conquerors, and they kept their word. Christians would never have dared to do this; they would have felt that it was tempting God.

But I err in speaking of a Christian republic; for each of these terms contradicts the other. Christianity preaches only servitude and submission. Its spirit is too favourable to tyranny for tyranny not to take advantage of it. True Christians are made to be slaves; they know it and they hardly care; this short life has too little value in their eyes.

It is said that Christian troops are excellent. I deny it. Show me these Christian troops. Personally I know of none. You may mention the crusades. But without disputing the valour of the crusaders, I shall say that they were far from being

Christians. They were soldiers of the priests. They were citizens of the Church; they were fighting for its spiritual homeland, which it had in some strange way made temporal. Strictly speaking, this comes under the heading of paganism; for since the Gospel never sets up any national religion, holy war is impossible among Christians.

Under the pagan Emperors, Christian soldiers were brave. All the Christian authors tell us this, and I believe them; but those soldiers were competing for honour against pagan troops. Once the Emperors became Christian, this emulation ceased; and once the cross had driven out the eagle, all Roman valour disappeared.

But leaving aside considerations of politics, let us return to those of right; and settle the principles which govern this important question. The right which the social pact gives the sovereign over the subjects does not, as I have said, go beyond the boundaries of public utility.* Subjects have no duty to account to the sovereign for their beliefs except when those beliefs are important to the community. Now it is very important to the state that each citizen should have a religion which makes him love his duty, but the dogmas of that religion are of interest neither to the state nor its members, except in so far as those dogmas concern morals and the duties which everyone who professes that religion is bound to perform towards others. Moreover, everyone may hold whatever opinions he pleases, without the sovereign having any business to take cognizance of them. For the sovereign has no compet-

* 'In the republic,' says the M(arquis) d'A(rgenson), 'everyone is perfectly free to do what does not injure others.' Here is the invariable boundary; one could not express it more exactly. I have not been able to deny myself the pleasure of quoting sometimes from this manuscript, although it is not known to the public, in order to pay homage to the memory of an illustrious and honourable man, who, even as a Minister of State, kept the heart of a true citizen, together with just and sound opinions on the government of his country.

ence in the other world; whatever may be the fate of the subjects in the life to come, it is nothing to do with the sovereign, so long as they are good citizens in this life.

There is thus a profession of faith which is purely civil and of which it is the sovereign's function to determine the articles, not strictly as religious dogmas, but as sentiments of sociability, without which it is impossible to be either a good citizen or a loyal subject.* Without being able to oblige anyone to believe these articles, the sovereign can banish from the state anyone who does not believe them; banish him not for impiety but as an antisocial being, as one unable sincerely to love law and justice, or to sacrifice, if need be, his life to his duty. If anyone, after having publicly acknowledged these same dogmas, behaves as if he did not believe in them, then let him be put to death, for he has committed the greatest crime, that of lying before the law.

The dogmas of the civil religion must be simple and few in number, expressed precisely and without explanations or commentaries. The existence of an omnipotent, intelligent, benevolent divinity that foresees and provides; the life to come; the happiness of the just; the punishment of sinners; the sanctity of the social contract and the law – these are the positive dogmas. As for the negative dogmas, I would limit them to a single one: no intolerance. Intolerance is something which belongs to the religions we have rejected.

In my opinion, those who distinguish between civil and theological intolerance are mistaken. These two forms of intolerance are inseparable. It is impossible to live in peace with people one believes to be damned; to love them would be to hate the God who punishes them; it is an absolute duty

* Caesar pleading for Catilina tried to establish the dogma of the mortality of the soul. Cato and Cicero, to refute it, did not waste time with philosophy; they were content to show that Caesar was speaking like a bad citizen and advancing a doctrine that was injurious to the state. And this was what the Senate had to give judgement on, not any question of theology.

either to redeem or to torture them. Wherever theological intolerance is admitted, it is bound to have some civil consequences,* and when it does so, the sovereign is no longer sovereign, even in the temporal sphere; at this stage the priests become the real masters, and kings are only their officers.

Now that there is not, and can no longer be, an exclusive national religion, all religions which themselves tolerate others must be tolerated, provided only that their dogmas contain nothing contrary to the duties of the citizen. But anyone who dares to say 'Outside the church there is no salvation' should be expelled from the state, unless the state is the church and the prince the pontiff. Such a dogma is good only in a theocratic government; in any other, it is pernicious. The reason for which Henri IV is said to have embraced the Catholic religion is one which should make all honest men abandon it, above all any prince who knows how to reason.

---

* Marriage, for example, being a civil contract, has civil consequences without which it would be impossible for society itself to subsist. Let us suppose that in a given country the clergy reached the point of gaining the sole right of permitting marriage, a right which it is bound to usurp under any intolerant religion. Is it not then clear that in making the authority of the church supreme in this matter, it will nullify that of the prince, who will then have no subjects other than those the clergy allow him to have? Enable priests to decide whether to marry people according to their assent to this or that doctrine, their assent to this or that formula, or according to their being more or less devout, then is it not clear that if the clergy acts shrewdly and holds firm, it will in time alone dispose of inheritances, offices, the citizens and the state itself, since the latter could not endure if composed only of bastards? But, you may say, men will call upon the temporal power, issue summonses and warrants, seize church properties. What a sorry sight! If the clergy has even a little, I do not say courage, but common sense, it will allow everything to go its own way; it will quietly let the summonses, the warrants and seizures take place and still end up as master. It is no great sacrifice, I feel, to give up a part when you are sure of securing the whole.

CHAPTER 9

Conclusion

AFTER setting out the true principles of political right, and trying to establish the state on the basis of those principles, I should complete my study by considering the foreign relations of the state, including the law of nations, commerce, the rights of war and conquest, international law, leagues, negotiations, treaties and so forth. But all this would represent a new subject too vast for my weak vision; and I would have had to keep my eyes fixed on matters within my range.

FOR THE BEST IN PAPERBACKS, LOOK FOR THE

In every corner of the world, on every subject under the sun, Penguin represents quality and variety – the very best in publishing today.

For complete information about books available from Penguin – including Pelicans, Puffins, Peregrines and Penguin Classics – and how to order them, write to us at the appropriate address below. Please note that for copyright reasons the selection of books varies from country to country.

In the United Kingdom: For a complete list of books available from Penguin in the U.K., please write to *Dept E.P., Penguin Books Ltd, Harmondsworth, Middlesex, UB7 0DA*

In the United States: For a complete list of books available from Penguin in the U.S., please write to *Dept BA, Penguin, 299 Murray Hill Parkway, East Rutherford, New Jersey 07073*

In Canada: For a complete list of books available from Penguin in Canada, please write to *Penguin Books Canada Ltd, 2801 John Street, Markham, Ontario L3R 1B4*

In Australia: For a complete list of books available from Penguin in Australia, please write to the *Marketing Department, Penguin Books Australia Ltd, P.O. Box 257, Ringwood, Victoria 3134*

In New Zealand: For a complete list of books available from Penguin in New Zealand, please write to the *Marketing Department, Penguin Books (NZ) Ltd, Private Bag, Takapuna, Auckland 9*

In India: For a complete list of books available from Penguin, please write to *Penguin Overseas Ltd, 706 Eros Apartments, 56 Nehru Place, New Delhi, 110019*

In Holland: For a complete list of books available from Penguin in Holland, please write to *Penguin Books Nederland B.V., Postbus 195, NL–1380AD Weesp, Netherlands*

In Germany: For a complete list of books available from Penguin, please write to *Penguin Books Ltd, Friedrichstrasse 10 – 12, D–6000 Frankfurt Main 1, Federal Republic of Germany*

In Spain: For a complete list of books available from Penguin in Spain, please write to *Longman Penguin España, Calle San Nicolas 15, E–28013 Madrid, Spain*

ROUSSEAU

THE CONFESSIONS

(*Translated by J. M. Cohen*)

In his posthumously published *Confessions* Jean-Jacques Rousseau (1712–78) describes the first fifty-three years of his life. With a frankness at times almost disconcerting, but always refreshing, he set out to reveal the whole truth about himself to the world, and succeeded in producing a masterpiece which has left its indelible imprint on the literature of successive generations, influencing among others Proust, Goethe, and Tolstoy.

J. M. Cohen's translation provides a clear, easy rendering in contemporary English of this fascinating panorama of eighteenth-century continental life, which ranges freely from the *haut monde* to the picaresque.

and

A DISCOURSE ON INEQUALITY

REVERIES OF THE SOLITARY WALKER

A Passage to India E. M. Forster

Centred on the unresolved mystery in the Marabar Caves, Forster's great work provides the definitive evocation of the British Raj.

The Republic Plato

The best-known of Plato's dialogues, *The Republic* is also one of the supreme masterpieces of Western philosophy whose influence cannot be overestimated.

The Life of Johnson James Boswell

Perhaps the finest 'life' ever written, Boswell's *Johnson* captures for all time one of the most colourful and talented figures in English literary history.

Remembrance of Things Past (3 volumes) Marcel Proust

This revised version by Terence Kilmartin of C. K. Scott Moncrieff's original translation has been universally acclaimed – available for the first time in paperback.

Metamorphoses Ovid

A golden treasury of myths and legends which has proved a major influence on Western literature.

A Nietzsche Reader Friedrich Nietzsche

A superb selection from all the major works of one of the greatest thinkers and writers in world literature, translated into clear, modern English.